# Henry IV, Part II SIMON CALLOW

Simon Callow trained at the Drama Centre and has been an actor since 1973. His roles include Arturo Ui, Titus in *Titus Andronicus*, Orlando in *As You Like It*, Mozart in the original production of *Amadeus*, Molina in *The Kiss of the Spider Woman*, Burgess/ Chubb in the world premiere of *Single Spies*, (RNT) which he also directed, Faust in *Faust* (parts one and two), Falstaff in *Chimes at Midnight*, *The Importance of Being Oscar* and *The Mystery of Charles Dickens* (World Premiere).

He has directed *The Infernal Machine* (Cocteau) with Maggie Smith, *Shirley Valentine* with Pauline Collins (West End and Broadway), *Les Enfants du Paradis* (RSC), *Die Fledermaus* (SO), *Carmen Jones* (Old Vic), *La Calisto* (Glimmerglass), *Il Trittico* (Broomhill), *Le Roi Malgré Lui* (??).

His books include *Being An Actor, Shooting The Actor, Love Is Where It Falls, The National, Acting in Restoration Comedy, Oscar Wilde and his Circle* and biographies of Orson Welles and Charles Laughton.

Simon Callow's previous book in the *Actors on Shakespeare* series was *Henry IV, Part I*.

Colin Nicholson is the originator and editor for the *Actors on Shakespeare* series published by Faber and Faber.

*in the same series*

# SIMON CALLOW

# Henry IV, Part II

*Series Editor: Colin Nicholson*

*faber and faber*

First published in 2003
by Faber and Faber Limited
3 Queen Square London WC1N 3AU

Typeset by Faber and Faber in Minion
Printed in England by Mackays of Chatham plc

The right of Simon Callow to be identified as author of this work has
been asserted in accordance with Section 77 of the Copyright, Designs
and Patents Act 1988

The right of Colin Nicholson to be identified as author of the
introduction has been asserted in accordance with Section 77 of the
Copyright, Designs and Patents Act 1988

A CIP record for this book is available from the British Library

ISBN 0–571–21628–5

10 9 8 7 6 5 4 3 2 1

ENL
R 588616

# Introduction

## Shakespeare: Playwright, Actor and Actors' Playwright

It is important to remember that William Shakespeare was an actor, and his understanding of the demands and rewards of acting helped him as a playwright to create roles of such richness and depth that actors in succeeding generations – even those with no reason or desire to call themselves 'classical' actors – have sought opportunities to perform them.

As the company dramatist, Shakespeare was writing under the pressure of producing scripts for almost immediate performance by his fellow players – the Lord Chamberlain's Men (later the King's Men), who, as a share-holding group, had a vested interest in their playhouse. Shakespeare was writing for a familiar set of actors: creating roles for particular players to interpret; and, being involved in a commercial enterprise, he was sensitive to the direct contact between player and audience and its power to bring in paying customers. His answer to the challenge produced a theatrical transformation: Shakespeare peopled the stage with highly credible personalities, men and women who were capable of change, and recognizable as participants in the human condition which their audience also shared. He connected two new and important elements: the idea of genuine individuality – the solitary, reflecting, self-communing soul, which is acutely aware of its own sufferings and desires; and, correlatively, the idea of inner life as something that not only exists but can also be explored. For him, the connection became the motor of dramatic action on the stage, as it is the motor of personal action in real life.

The primary importance of the actor cannot be disputed: it is his or her obligation – assisted to a greater or lesser extent by a director's overall vision of the play – to understand the personality they are representing onstage, and the nature of the frictions taking place when that personality interacts with other characters in the drama. Shakespeare's achievement goes far beyond the creation of memorable characters (Macbeth, Falstaff) to embrace the exposition of great relationships (Macbeth–Lady Macbeth; Falstaff–Prince Hal). Great roles require great actors, and there is no group of people in a better position to interpret those roles to *us* than the principal actors of *our* generation – inhabitants of a bloodline whose vigour resonates from the sixteenth century to the present day – who have immersed themselves in the details of Shakespeare's creations and have been party to their development through rehearsal and performance.

Watching Shakespeare can be an intimidating experience, especially for those who are not well versed in the text, or in the conventions of the Elizabethan stage. Many excellent books have been written for the academic market but our aim in this series is somewhat different. *Actors on Shakespeare* asks contemporary performers to choose a play of particular interest to them, push back any formal boundaries that may obstruct channels of free communication and give the modern audience a fresh, personal view. Naturally the focus for each performer is different – and these diverse volumes are anything but uniform in their approach to the task – but their common intention is, primarily, to look again at plays that some audiences may know well and others not at all, as well as providing an insight into the making of a performance.

Each volume works in its own right, without assuming an in-depth knowledge of the play, and uses substantial quotation to contextualize the principal points. The fresh approach of the many and varied writers will, we hope, enhance your enjoyment of Shakespeare's work.

Colin Nicholson

February 2002

**Note:** For reference, the text used here is
the Arden Shakespeare.

# Characters

**At Court**
King Henry IV
Henry, Prince of Wales
Prince John of Lancaster
Westmoreland
Blunt

IN PART II ONLY
Clarence, Gloucester, Warwick, Kent, Surrey
Lord Chief Justice
Gower, Harcourt

**Rebels**
Earl of Northumberland
Harry Percy ('Hotspur')

IN PART I ONLY
Worcester
Douglas
Owen Glendower
Mortimer (Earl of March)
Vernon
Glendower's Wife

IN PART II ONLY
Lords Bardolph, Hastings, Mowbray, Coleville, Falconbridge,
   Blunt
Lady Northumberland
Travers, Morton

**From the Boar's Head Tavern**
Sir John Falstaff
Mistress Quickly
Bardolph
Peto
Poins
Nym
Francis, *the drawer*

IN PART I ONLY
Chamberlain
Gadshill

IN PART II ONLY
Pistol
Doll Tearsheet
Falstaff's page

**In Gloucestershire**
PART II ONLY
Justice Shallow
Justice Silence
Davy
Bullcalf, Feeble, Mouldy, Shadow, Wart, *recruits*

**Others**
Lords, Ladies, Officers, Soldiers, Messengers, Musicians

IN PART I ONLY
Carriers, Travellers, Sheriff

IN PART II ONLY
Beadles, Drawer, Fang, Grooms
Rumour *as prologue*
Second Porter, Snare

*Chimes at Midnight* (a play drawn from *Henry IV, Parts I* and *II*) was performed at the Chichester Festival Theatre in August 1998 with the following cast:

| | |
|---|---|
| Chorus/ Lord Chief Justice | Michael G. Jones |
| King Henry IV | Keith Baxter |
| Northumberland/ Justice Shallow | Timothy Bateson |
| Earl of Worcester/ Pistol | David Cardy |
| Harry Hotspur/ Attendant to Lord Chief Justice | Tristan Gemmill |
| Earl of Westmoreland | Rowland Davies |
| John of Lancaster | Sebastian Warrack |
| Prince Hal | Tam Williams |
| Sir John Falstaff | Simon Callow |
| Poins/ Wart | Simon Prestage |
| Lady Percy/ Doll Tearsheet | Rebecca Egan |
| Bardolph | David Weston |
| Peto/ Feeble | Adrian Rigelsford |
| Mistress Quickly | Sarah Badel |
| Sheriff Fang/ Silence | John Warner |
| Snare/ Shadow/ Traveller | Roger Braban |
| Mouldy/ Nym | Timothy Wright |
| Davy/ Gower/ Traveller | Gary Richards |
| Nun/ Traveller/ Wench | Alexandra Lilley |
| Attendant to Hotspur/ Wench | Amanda Holmes |
| Soldier and Lord | Adam James |

*Directed by* Patrick Garland

To the memory of an incomparable teacher, Yat Malmgren (1916–2002), whose inspiration to his thousands of students burns bright in their work and lives, and for Christopher Fettes, continuing inspiration.

# The Story So Far

Prince Henry, heir to the throne, having been dismissed by the King and the court for his low-lifing ways, has rallied to his father's side to defeat the rebellion led by Harry Percy ('the Hotspur of the North') and his family. At the climax of the Battle of Shrewsbury he slays Hotspur heroically in single combat. His carousing companion, the irrepressible elderly reprobate Sir John Falstaff, has falsely taken credit for the death of Hotspur, and *Henry IV, Part I* ends with promises of reform on the part of Falstaff, of further action against the rebels on the part of the King, and the expectation that the young Prince ('Hal', as Falstaff calls him) will take his place at the side of his father, ready to assume the crown whenever necessary.

For those who have just joined us, much of the Prelude to the companion volume on *Henry IV, Part I* was concerned with considering the complex weave of elements in that play, and the essential strands remain the same in *Part II*: the breakdown of feudal society in the face of the centralizing tendency of the crown, manifested in the conflict between the Northern barons and the King (the former Henry Bolingbroke, usurper of the throne of Richard II); the rites of passage of Prince Harry in his journey towards manhood and kingship; the realistic portrayal of modern Elizabethan life, especially in the low-life scenes; and the glorious anomaly of the huge, semi-pagan figure who to such a large extent dominates both plays and impinges on both worlds, political and personal: the Fat Knight himself, Falstaff. This variegated texture is precisely evoked by the scholar Graham Holderness in his observation that in the plays 'a chivalric medieval prince could meet a band of 16th-century soldiers led by a figure from immemorial carnival'. I tried to investigate the ways in which these strands work in the theatre. I was particularly engaged by the carnival and ritual aspects of the play, and was of the view articulated by C. L. Barber that in *Part I* 'Falstaff reigns, within his sphere, as carnival,' while *Part II* – which we now address – 'is very largely taken up with his trial'. To put it another way, it is Falstaff's disreputable vitality that colours the first play, and it is his decline and dismissal that pervade the second.

There is much animated scholarly debate about whether the two parts of *Henry IV* were conceived as 'one long ten-act play' or as two separate plays of normal duration. Did Shakespeare know that there would be a *Part II* when he was writing *Part I*? Can either part stand on its own? In particular, does *Part I* really come to a full close? Much of this discussion is in the most literal sense academic, but when the plays are played – as increasingly often – together on one day, or on consecutive nights, there is a serious difficulty that presents major challenges to directors and actors. I will be considering this later in the book. Meanwhile, to reproduce the last paragraph of my earlier volume on *Part I*: '[The King] ends the play with ringing determination:

> Rebellion in this land shall lose his sway,
> Meeting the check of such another day,
> And since this business so fair is done,
> Let us not leave till all our own be done.

Much, however, remains to be resolved: the matter of *Henry IV, Part II*. Will the King's relationship with Hal continue to grow? Will he extinguish the rebels? Will he send an army to the crusades? And will Falstaff settle down, as he promised, and go on a diet? We are agog to find out the answers to all these cliff-hanging questions, just as our author intended.'

# Induction

## Warkworth. Before Northumberland's castle

The location, as Lady Bracknell might say, is immaterial. We are in a theatre, being addressed by an actor impersonating Rumour – a figure familiar to Elizabethan audiences from his appearances, arrayed in tongues, in the interludes and pageants of the previous reign. He knows that what he has to tell us is irresistible: 'for which of you will stop / The vent of hearing when loud Rumour speaks?' In fact, his attitude to his audience verges on the contemptuous: having described the way in which 'the blunt monster with uncounted heads / The still-discordant wav'ring multitude' – in other words, us – plays on the stops of Rumour's pipes, he asks,

> But what need I thus
> My well-known body to anatomize
> Among my household?

We, it seems, are part of his family. True to his nature, he proceeds to give us the opposite of the truth, though he knows perfectly well what really happened: Hal fell, he says, to Hotspur's sword; the King was killed by Douglas. With malicious delight he notes that messengers are descending from all quarters on Northumberland's castle 'and not a man of them brings other news / Than they have learnt of me'. The Induction serves as a lively and quirky fanfare for the play proper, and its mischievous levity contrasts strikingly with the grim and violent emotions of Rumour's victims.

## Act One

**Scene i: Warkworth. Before Northumberland's castle**

In an opening of high urgency, the unhappily named Lord Bardolph (the name is historical, but it is surely unfortunate that Shakespeare should have duplicated such uncommon nomenclature) demands to see Northumberland, Hotspur's father, and the nominal leader of the rebels, earlier denounced by Hotspur for failing to make his promised appearance at the battle of Shrewsbury, on grounds of sickness. Rumour now describes him as 'crafty-sick'. (But can we trust anything Rumour says?) Lord Bardolph, who has been well instructed by Rumour, tells Northumberland – himself in a highly charged state, his anxiety no doubt intensified by guilt at having abandoned his fellow-rebels – news 'as good as heart could wish'. The King is close to death, Hal slain by Hotspur; the young princes have fled the field, and Falstaff ('Harry Monmouth's brawn' – the meaty images by which he is so often characterized in both the plays serve to introduce him in the second part) is taken prisoner. Northumberland immediately wants to know whether this report can be trusted; and no sooner does his own emissary Travers appear, than Bardolph's reassurances crumble. Travers has encountered a gentleman racing from the battlefield who told him that 'rebellion had ill luck' and, he reports with artless bluntness, that 'young Harry Percy's spur was cold'. With distracted horror, Northumberland repeats this dark pun on his son's nickname:

Ha? Again!
Said he young Harry Percy's spur was cold?

Of Hotspur, Coldspur? that rebellion
Had met ill luck?

Lord Bardolph insists on his version of events, only to be gain-said by Morton, whose face tells Northumberland all he needs to know: '. . . this man's brow, like to a title-leaf / Foretells the nature of a tragic volume.' Morton has come direct from Shrewsbury, 'Where hateful death put on his ugliest mask / To fright our party.' The scene is of terrible intensity, as Northumberland tells us when he describes the messenger with his grim news:

Thou tremblest, and the whiteness in thy cheek
Is apter than thy tongue to tell thy errand.
Even such a man, so faint, so spiritless,
So dull, so dead in look, so woe-begone,
Drew Priam's curtain in the dead of night . . .

Recent events in America, widely televised, in which over and over again dreaded news has been broken to desperate and terrified relatives, torn between hope and despair, gives some sense of the emotional level of this scene. Northumberland teeters between certainty that Hotspur is dead and a longing to be contradicted, and Lord Bardolph persists in giving him false hope; but Morton will have none of it. Doggedly he compels Northumberland to accept the truth:

I am sorry I should force you to believe
That which I would to God I had not seen;
But these mine eyes saw him in bloody state,
Rend'ring faint quittance, wearied and out-breath'd,
To Harry Monmouth, whose swift wrath beat down
The never-daunted Percy to the earth,
From whence with life he never more sprung up.

Relentlessly he describes the consequent abandonment of the field by Hotspur's troops:

> For from his metal was his party steel'd,
> Which once in him abated, all the rest
> Turn'd on themselves like dull and heavy lead.

Finally, this truth-teller informs Northumberland that Prince John and Westmoreland are on their way to confront the old man.

Northumberland's grief takes him to the edge of insanity. Hurling aside his crutch and throwing off his nightcap, he cries for a collapse of the natural order and an end of human life:

> ... let one spirit of the first-born Cain
> Reign in all bosoms, that, each heart being set
> On bloody courses, the rude scene may end,
> And darkness be the burier of the dead!

This is Hitler in the bunker, and even Lord Bardolph and Morton are disturbed by the wanton nihilism of it. Morton reminds Northumberland that he joined the rebellion in the clear knowledge that defeat and death were the possible outcome, and that Hotspur in particular was most likely to meet his end on the battlefield. Rallying his confederates, he brings news of the Archbishop of York's commitment to their cause, an event that transforms their position: his renowned holiness and authority legitimize the rebellion, a word that has hitherto made potential supporters anxious – that

> froze them up,
> As fish are in a pond. But now the Bishop
> Turns insurrection to religion.

Northumberland is finally recovered sufficiently to report that he knew of this, but his griefs have distracted him; now he swings back into action. 'Get posts and letters and make friends with speed: / Never so few, and never yet more need.'

This opening scene strikes notes that will often be heard. Northumberland's sickness itself is the first of many throughout the course of the play, in which England sometimes seems to be dying on its feet. The proud chivalric strain that characterized the scenes with the Percys in *Henry IV, Part I* is muted and turned to recrimination, despair and a sense of spiritual defeat. The idea for which they stood no longer inspires them; it is mere survival that matters, and – as in Northumberland's terrible outburst: 'Let order die!' – there is an atmosphere of universal doom. The death throes of the rebellion are graphically delineated: an ugly and sometimes pitiable sight, as the dinosaurs wheel and stagger. It is worth noting that the role of Morton (and this is the full extent of it) requires a particularly strong actor: he, the messenger of doom, also has to take a hold of two partners who are, in the one case, idiotically deluded, and in the other, in the grip of overwhelming and nearly self-annihilating emotions. By dint of utter realism and calm analysis, he transforms the scene from one of destructive emotion into one of practical action.

### Scene ii: London. A street

Falstaff has been taking some practical action of his own: a visit to the doctor. After the anguish and desperation of the previous scene, Falstaff, on his return to the stage, is characteristically concerned with his bodily functions: '. . . what says the doctor to my water?' He now has a Page (given to him, we later discover, by Hal), with whom he creates a very effective double act. It is notable that Falstaff is not purely a comic monologist (though he is a very good one of those), but also excels in setting up a bantering relationship with one or more others, whom he turns into comic foils, endowing them with qualities that he either exaggerates or invents out of thin air. His Page – presumably originally a small boy in the acting company – becomes 'you giant' and serves as an admirable counterpoint to his own vastness, which he alternately glories in and laments. Today he feels – or pretends to feel – put upon: even the doctor makes a joke at his expense; but then, who doesn't? 'I am not only witty in myself,' he says, 'but the cause that wit is in other men.' His sense of self is so overpowering that he sees himself as the source of all things. He broods on his girth, whimsically convinced that Hal has given him this diminutive Page only 'to set [him] off'. When he describes himself, it is still in the language of livestock, but with an interesting variant: he defines himself in terms of a female animal. 'I do here walk before thee like a sow that hath overwhelmed all her litter but one.' Indeed there is, as we have remarked in commenting on *Henry IV, Part I*, something of the Earth Mother about Falstaff, like an Easter Island figure. His patter – for that is what it is – takes in Hal's beardlessness, accusing him (with no evidence whatever) of boasting about his manliness. He weaves these majestic disquisitions out of the thinnest material, but the intellectual vitality and inventiveness are inexhaustible, as he sounds every note in his personality, from the profane to the mock-pious, taking in surreal speculations ('. . . thou art fitter to be worn in my cap than to wait at my heels') and elaborate and many-layered puns, mostly to do with coinage, and mostly, alas, lost to us in theatrical practice, however ingeniously the editors explain them.

An enquiry as to the progress of his new clothes – appropriate to his newly honoured state – reveals that the tailor will not accept his security, which elicits a virtuoso denunciation of the very concept – at least in relation to him. A typical instance of the Falstaffian thought process occurs during the grumbling winding-down of his assault on the nefarious tailor, whom he accuses of cuckoldry, 'for he hath the horn of abundance, and the lightness of his wife shines through it; and yet cannot he see, though he have his own lanthorn to light him. Where's Bardolph?' The ability of Bardolph's nose to shine in the dark has been well established in *Henry IV, Part I*; Falstaff's instant association is richly comic in itself.

The stand-up comedy is interrupted by the appearance of the Lord Chief Justice, a formidable figure, certain enough of his own authority, we discover, to have imprisoned Hal for striking him during some earlier escapade. When he finds that he is in the presence of Falstaff, he immediately recalls the robbery at Gadshill from the earlier play; Falstaff, naturally, is eager to avoid this conversation. 'Boy, tell him I am deaf.' The Lord Chief Justice's servant moves to apprehend him, and Falstaff performs one of his virtuoso feats of inversion – treating the servant as if he were a beggar, which provokes volleys of mock-disapproval. The servant is admirably unfazed and brings Falstaff into the Lord Chief Justice's presence, who without preamble attempts to raise the matter of Falstaff's failure to appear before him after the robbery. Falstaff relentlessly pursues an entirely different matter: the King's health, of which he speaks with detailed knowledge, all the while working himself up into a provocative impertinence. The King's apoplexy – paralysis – he says, is caused, according to Galen, by 'a kind of deafness'. 'I think you are fallen into the disease,' says the exasperated Lord Chief Justice, 'for you hear not what I say to you.' No, says Falstaff; it's just that I'm not listening. For every challenge the lawman offers him, Falstaff has another piece of effrontery, including a number of vintage music-hall jokes:

LORD CHIEF JUSTICE Your means are very slender, and your waste is great.

FALSTAFF I would it were otherwise, I would my means were greater and my waist slenderer.

The burden of the Lord Chief Justice's complaint, and the reason for the urgency of his interrogation of Falstaff, is simple: 'You have misled the youthful Prince.' Falstaff's reply to this, though obscure in meaning – perhaps it refers to a proverb or a popular stage character lost to us – is highly suggestive: 'The young Prince hath misled me. I am the fellow with the great belly, and he my dog.' The *lèse-majesté* is breathtaking, but it also paints a picture of co-dependence, of two creatures belonging to each other. It certainly arrests the Lord Chief Justice in his tracks; he is prepared to forget the Gadshill incident; but Falstaff will not leave well alone, and the Lord Chief Justice starts to trade crude insults with him. Of course, only Falstaff can win this sort of a contest. Accused of being a burnt-out candle, he rather compares himself to a wassail candle – associating himself yet again with animal fat and with pagan tradition; bemoans the cynicism and cupidity of the present age; turns on their head the Lord Chief Justice's admonitions to him to behave with the dignity appropriate to his years – 'Have you not a moist eye, a dry hand, a yellow cheek, a white beard, a decreasing leg, an increasing belly?' – 'My lord, I was born about three of the clock in the afternoon, with a white head, and something a round belly'; laments the reliance of the nation on his valour in battle – 'I would to God my name were not so terrible to the enemy as it is – I were better to be eaten to death with a rust than to be scoured to nothing with perpetual motion'; and finally tries to borrow a thousand pounds from the Lord Chief Justice.

It is as great a triumph of sheer mischief and avoidance as Falstaff ever achieves in either of the plays – inventive, anarchic, nimble, hilarious; but when the scene is over, he sinks into a somewhat melancholy survey of his situation. And here it appears that even his purse has succumbed to the sickness that invades every aspect of the play's world. 'I can get no remedy against this consumption of the purse; borrowing only lingers and lingers it out, but the disease is incurable.' He despatches his Page with letters to Hal, to Prince John, to Westmoreland and finally to Mistress Ursula (who may or may not be Mistress Quickly), whom he intends to continue to encourage in the belief that he will marry her. A stab of pain in his toe reminds him of his physical ailments: 'A pox of this gout! or a gout of this pox!'; but even pox can be turned to advantage: he can get a war pension for it. 'A good wit will make use of anything; I will turn diseases to commodity.'

Falstaff ascendant, then. Not as well off as he'd like to be, not as *well* as he'd like to be, but surviving triumphantly on his wits, to his own great satisfaction, and ours – but with one crucial difference: he is not with Hal. The Lord Chief Justice reminds him that he has been sent on a different campaign from Hal's; he is with John of Lancaster. When the Lord Chief Justice cries: 'God send the Prince a better companion!', he replies: 'God send the companion a better prince!' and adds, 'I cannot rid my hands of him.' It is oddly hollow: Falstaff is Falstaff yet, but something is missing.

### Scene iii: York. The Archbishop's palace

The Archbishop of York, that holy, scholarly man, is taking counsel with his partners in rebellion. Significantly, Northumberland is absent, and his participation in the enterprise is again cause for anxiety. Lord Bardolph, who emerges as a serious if cautious thinker, warns against rash optimism:

> For in a theme so bloody-fac'd as this
> Conjecture, expectation, and surmise
> Of aids incertain should not be admitted.

The Archbishop reminds his partners of the dreadful example of Hotspur, whom Lord Bardolph vividly recalls: he

> lin'd himself with hope,
> Eating the air and promise of supply,
> Flatt'ring himself in project of a power
> Much smaller than the smallest of his thoughts,
> And so, with great imagination
> Proper to madmen, led his powers to death,
> And winking leap'd into destruction.

So much for heroism. Lord Bardolph continues the elaboration of his cautious approach, comparing the apparent strength of their position to an early spring when

> We see th'appearing buds; which to prove fruit
> Hope gives not so much warrant, as despair
> That frosts will bite them.

His steady tone does not signify lack of ambition; his definition of their enterprise – 'this great work' – is nothing if not visionary: '. . . almost to pluck a kingdom down / And set another up'; but in a long and magisterially worked out metaphor he insists that

> When we mean to build,
> We first survey the plot, then draw the model,
> And when we see the figure of the house,
> Then must we rate the cost of the erection,

Which if we find outweighs ability,
What do we then but draw anew the model
In fewer offices, or at least desist
To build at all?

If not, they (the rebels) are

Like one that draws the model of an house
Beyond his power to build it, who, half-through,
Gives o'er, and leaves his part-created cost
A naked subject to the weeping clouds,
And waste for churlish winter's tyranny.

This magisterial analysis is neither answered nor swept aside, but Hastings persists in believing that they have cause for confidence; even without Northumberland they have 25,000 men, as many as the 'unfirm' King, who is, moreover, fighting on three fronts, his exchequer empty. The Archbishop is persuaded: 'Let us on, / And publish the occasion of our arms.' In a lurid image dense with distaste and patrician contempt, he observes that the King has lost the love of the gormandizing people, 'O thou fond many,' the 'beastly feeder' that

art so full of him
That thou provok'st thyself to cast him up.
So, so, thou common dog, didst thou disgorge
Thy glutton bosom of the royal Richard;
And now thou wouldst eat thy dead vomit up,
And howlst to find it.

The overwhelming disgust, not only with the people but with the times themselves, is the characteristic note of this scene. 'O thoughts of men accurs'd! / Past and to come seems best; things present, worst.' Nowhere is there any statement of

the ideal that drives the conspirators on – not even an assertion of family pride; the well-being of the despised people is
the last of their considerations. There is simply the irresistible
compulsion to eliminate the hated King. They seem even to
have forgotten why they hate him; and they move forward
simply because they have to: 'We are time's subjects, and time
bids be gone.' The bleakness is unrelieved.

# Act Two

## Scene i: Eastcheap. Near the Boar's Head Tavern

Things are turning pretty sour among the low-lifers, too. Mistress Quickly has enlisted two officers of the law, Fang and Snare, to apprehend Falstaff. The cause is ostensibly the reclamation of the outstanding sums of money that he owes her, but there is another, more personal grievance: his failure to marry her. Snare, Fang's yeoman, expresses anxiety: 'It may chance cost some of us our lives, for he will stab.' It is clear that Falstaff is well known for fighting dirty; nor are women safe. Mistress Quickly tells us that he stabbed her in her own house. 'A cares not what mischief he does, if his weapon be out.' It is in this scene of the play that Mistress Quickly's unique voice is first heard in all its inimitable glory, mounting raids on the English language, lungeing at sense, compounding phrases, recklessly neologizing, saying rather more than she means, though often hitting the nail on the head – as here. Sir John's weapon, in the anatomical sense, is indeed a menace to all: '. . . he will spare neither man, woman, nor child'; but she is no mere Malaprop. Her speech is richly eloquent, rhetorical and impassioned:

> A hundred mark is a long one for a poor lone woman to bear, and I have borne, and borne, and borne, and have been fubbed off, and fubbed off, and fubbed off, from this day to that day, that it is a shame to be thought on. There is no honesty in such dealing, unless a woman should be made an ass, and a beast, to bear every knave's wrong.

It is under pressure that her language bursts and buckles; as it does with the arrival of Falstaff, who, the moment they try to apprehend him, cries, with conspicuous ungallantry, 'Throw the quean in the channel!' She does not trouble to rebut the allegation that she is a tart – it would perhaps be too hard a case to make – but indignantly howls,

> Throw me in the channel? I'll throw thee in the channel.
> Wilt thou, wilt thou, thou bastardly rogue? Murder!
> Murder! Ah, thou honeysuckle villain, wilt thou kill God's
> officers and the King's? Ah, thou honeyseed rogue! Thou
> art a honeyseed, a man queller, and a woman queller!

No doubt she intends to call Falstaff a homicide, as A. R. Humphreys suggests, but 'honeyseed rogue' is a perfectly apt description of him: seedy, honeyed, a rogue.

Falstaff, meanwhile, in full accord with his usual impulses, is busy urging Bardolph to defend him; the tiny Page joins in, hurling abuse around quite as energetically as his seniors – 'you rampallian! you fustilarian! I'll tickle your catastrophe!' – as the officers call for help. At this point in the mayhem, the Lord Chief Justice returns with his men. His stern attempts to restore order are baffled as much by the aggrieved party as by the accused. Asking Mistress Quickly, 'For what sum?' he is answered, 'It is more than for some, my lord, it is for all I have.' The severe lawman finds himself in the midst not only of a brawl, but of a music-hall sketch. Quickly continues with her petition: if she doesn't get some of what she has put into 'that fat belly of his', she will 'ride [him] a-nights like the mare' – that is, give him nightmares. Falstaff naturally picks up on the sexual connotation of the word 'ride'. The Lord Chief Justice impatiently upbraids him for his abuse of this 'poor widow'; but on Falstaff's enquiry as to how much he's supposed to owe, the underlying grievance wells up:

Thou didst swear to me upon a parcel-gilt goblet, sitting in my Dolphin chamber, at the round table, by a sea-coal fire, upon Wednesday in Wheeson week, when the Prince broke thy head for liking his father to a singing-man of Windsor – thou didst swear to me then, as I was washing thy wound, to marry me, and make me my lady thy wife.

Here a further dimension of Mistress Quickly emerges: her undiscriminating recall of everything that she sees and has ever seen, which pours forth in a Joycean stream – or rather, flood – of consciousness: the precise goblet, the particular room, the kind of coal, the specific day in Whitsun. This is a quality she shares with the Nurse in *Romeo And Juliet*, but Quickly's brain is in greater flux than the Nurse's. Recollections come tumbling out, jostling each other, as her memory seems to haemorrhage:

Canst thou deny it? Did not goodwife Keech the butcher's wife come in then and call me gossip Quickly? – coming in to borrow a mess of vinegar, telling us she had a good dish of prawns, whereby thou didst desire to eat some, whereby I told thee they were ill for a green wound? And didst thou not, when she was gone downstairs, desire me to be no more so familiarity with such poor people, saying that ere long they should call me madam?

The circumstantial evidence is, for her, proof positive of her testimony; and indeed it has at every level the ring of truth, particularly Falstaff's coup de grâce, as she reports it: 'And didst thou not kiss me, and bid me fetch thee thirty shillings? I put thee now to thy book oath, deny it if thou canst.' This is life as it is lived: the neighbour coming in with her prawns, wanting some vinegar to season them; Falstaff fancying a bite (but Quickly protectively – and perhaps jealously – stopping

19

him from having one), then bad-mouthing the neighbour as soon as she's left the room.

Her account of the initial incident that led to the intimacy of her dressing Falstaff's head wound, which seems to have led directly to his proposal to her, gives a sudden glimpse of his relationship with Hal, of which we have heard so little in *Henry IV, Part II* so far – a revealing and rare moment of Hal rebelling against Falstaff's *lèse-majesté*. Falstaff has accused the King of being 'a singing-man of Windsor' – a reference to an impostor who substituted for Richard II – in effect, as Humphreys has said, accusing the King of being falsely enthroned. Clearly this had been too close to the bone for Hal.

As for Quickly's detailed reconstruction of Falstaff's proposal to her, he will have none of it and outrageously shifts the focus on to the Lord Chief Justice himself.

> My lord, this is a poor mad soul, and she says up and
> down the town that her eldest son is like you. She hath
> been in good case, and the truth is, poverty hath distracted
> her. But for these foolish officers, I beseech you I may have
> redress against them.

The lawman is not to be deflected:

> Sir John, Sir John, I am well acquainted with your manner
> of wrenching the true cause the false way. It is not a confi-
> dent brow, nor the throng of words that come with such
> more than impudent sauciness from you, can thrust me
> from a level consideration.

After rallying once more, Falstaff obeys him and takes Quickly to one side, emerging with the phrase: 'As I am a gentleman!' Obviously no cash will be forthcoming, and she will have to sell her household effects; but Falstaff has clearly won, and with characteristic legerdemain, turns the tables on her, forgiving her for her bad behaviour with lordly magnanimity, using those affectionate and intimate means by which he steals so many hearts: 'Come, and 'twere not for thy humours, there's not a better wench in England. Go, wash thy face, and draw the action. Come, thou must not be in this humour with me, dost not know me?' He is still intent on his thirty shillings. When she offers resistance, he threatens to go else-where, and finally she submits. To her tentative enquiry: 'You'll pay me all together?' he roars, 'Will I live?', and it might be the defining phrase of his existence: his vitality is his essence. As if in acknowledgement of that, she arranges for her resident whore, Doll Tearsheet, to be available to him. The mind reels at the thought of what a marriage between Falstaff and Quickly might consist of.

Meanwhile the cold reality of the political world invades the woozy, blurred, explosive and all-too-human world of Eastcheap: Gower appears with urgent and troubling news of the campaign ahead. Falstaff expects to be informed of the latest developments. The Lord Chief Justice pointedly excludes him, reproaching him for dallying when there are soldiers to be recruited; but Falstaff has even more urgent business in mind: supper. He invites Gower to join him – and the thought of that potentate settling down into the stews of the Boar's Head is a mind-boggling one – but there is no question of it. The Lord Chief Justice for once has the last word: 'Now the Lord lighten thee; thou art a great fool.' For all his comic bravado, it is hard to avoid the sense that events are passing Falstaff by.


### Scene ii: London. A room in the Prince's house

It is only now, a third of the way into the play, that Hal appears, and when he does it is in a strikingly different mood from the one in which we left him at the end of *King Henry IV, Part I*, apparently reformed, a hero and loyal lieutenant to his father, poised for greatness. 'Before God, I am exceeding weary,' he says. He is with the companion of his low-life exploits, Poins, whose presence has never graced any battlefield, and their banter, though familiar, is curiously off-key. Hal seems to have relapsed into a state of self-disgust and disgust with the life he leads. This includes his relationship with Poins: 'What a disgrace it is to me to remember thy name!' Something of their intimacy is revealed in Hal's curious recitation of Poins's linen:

> . . . how many pair of silk stockings thou hast – viz. these, and those that were thy peach-coloured ones! or to bear the inventory of thy shirts – as, one for superfluity, and another for use!

There is, of course, a sting in the tail:

> But that the tennis-court keeper knows better than I, for it is a low ebb of linen with thee when thou keepest not racket there; as thou hast not done a great while, because the rest of thy low countries have made a shift to eat up thy holland. And God knows whether those that bawl out the ruins of thy linen shall inherit his kingdom: but the midwives say the children are not in the fault; whereupon the world increases, and kindreds are mightily strengthened.

Poins has been fathering bastards: his 'low countries' – nether regions – have been wearing out the linen ('holland'). It is to be assumed that these bastards have been sired in the same stews as Poins and Hal frequent together; the tone suggests a mingled revulsion and fascination that is perhaps a clue to the young Prince's apparent recidivism, and to the famous structural difficulty of *Henry IV, Part II*. It is as if Shakespeare and Hal have both forgotten what happened at the end of the earlier play, as if we were back to the juvenile delinquent Hal of Gadshill, and the heroic activities of Shrewsbury Plain and the heartening reconciliation with the King his father were dreams or fantasies.

There is no question that if the two plays are taken as one, there is a structural oddity. Particularly when the two plays are shown consecutively, on a single day (as never happened in Shakespeare's time, of course), it is as if one had missed something, some turn of the plot. There is no hint by the end of *Henry IV, Part I* that Hal is anything other than a new man, unless perhaps one takes into account his affectionate and tolerant attitude to Falstaff, an attitude that, the events of the present play will clearly insist, is incompatible with his royal status. The nature of *Part II*, however, is radically different from that of *Part I*, often revisiting the themes and situations of the earlier play from a different angle, coming at it, as it were, from a different perspective. What L. C. Knights so suggestively says of Falstaff's first appearance in *Part II* applies to the whole play: 'He seems, at first perplexingly, to be both the same figure as before and yet another: it is as though we had given a further twist to the screw of our binoculars and what we thought we knew has appeared more sharply defined against a background that he no longer dominated.' There is more to be known about Hal, and the playwright happily sacrifices linearity of narrative for his further explorations.

From a psychological perspective, it is deeply convincing that a transformation secured by the adrenalin of battle should not have fully taken – that Hal's slow journey towards kingship and maturity has several more stages before that destination is reached. There is still unfinished business in Eastcheap, to do with nether regions both spiritual and

23

physical; and, of course, the question of Falstaff and Hal's addiction to him is still outstanding. There is, too, the existential matter, the elusive sense of being: Hamlet-like, the Prince is able to play successive roles while seeming not to have an identity of his own. Who is he? And who is he required to be? What is he required to feel? And what does he really feel? Despite his recent firework display of valour on the field of war, he still feels inadequate for the role he was born to play, the greatest role of all in the pageant of English history. These feelings of inadequacy arise because, far from being frivolous and contemptuous of his father, as his detractors maintain, he is deeply serious, profoundly conscious, not only of the greatness of the challenge before him, but also of the greatness of his father. Poins, feeling perhaps that Hal's sexually charged banter has come dangerously close to hostility, goes straight for the jugular, a move entirely in character:

> How ill it follows, after you have laboured so hard, you should talk so idly! Tell me, how many good young princes would do so, their fathers being so sick as yours at this time is.

Hal's defence is a complex one: 'my heart bleeds inwardly that my father is so sick,' he says, but it would be inappropriate for him to express his feelings in Poins's company because he would be thought to be a hypocrite – 'a most princely hypocrite', as Poins puts it.

Hal's reply is a useful clue as to why he cultivates Poins's company:

> It would be every man's thought; and thou art a blessed fellow, to think as every man thinks. Never a man's thought in the world keeps the roadway better than thine: every man would think me an hypocrite indeed.

Poins is Hal's vox pop; he is as ordinary as Falstaff is exceptional. Between them, they are a complete education in real life.

An emissary of Falstaff now appears: '... the boy that I gave Falstaff – a had him from me Christian, and look if the fat villain have not transformed him ape.' He is accompanied by Bardolph, hailed, not without irony but with the courtesy that Hal usually offers to his subordinates, as 'most noble Bardolph!' This heroic toper now comes in for his usual ritual abuse, harping on the redness of his features; even the Page, aping – as Hal might say – his master, launches into an elaborate satire on the sottish subaltern:

A calls me e'en now, my lord, through a red lattice, and I could discern no part of his face from the window. At last I spied his eyes, and methought he had made two holes in the ale-wife's new petticoat, and so peeped through.

Much banter ensues, into which Hal enters with apparent pleasure; a letter from Falstaff brings more matter for mirth. The content of the letter is stupendously mischievous, however, accusing Poins of trying to secure a match between his sister and Hal, a shocking thought, which he shiftily denies: 'God send the wench no worse fortune! But I never said so.' Hal determines to spy on Falstaff at Eastcheap ('Doth the old boar feed in the old frank?') and enquires somewhat lubriciously about his female companionship. 'This Doll Tearsheet should be some road,' he suggests to Poins when they are alone. 'I warrant you,' is the reply, 'as common as the way between Saint Albans and London.' Poins proposes that they should disguise themselves as waiters the better to spy on them, which suggestion Hal takes up with a certain bitter relish. It seems entirely fitting to him, in his present mood of self-contempt:

From a god to a bull? A heavy descension! It was Jove's
case. From a prince to a prentice? A low transformation,
that shall be mine, for in everything the purpose must
weigh with the folly. Follow me, Ned.

## Scene iii: Warkworth. Northumberland's castle

While Hal vacillates over his destiny at a far remove from
the war, that dinosaur Northumberland is also paralysed by
indecision, also distant from the fighting. Both his wife and
his daughter-in-law, Hotspur's widow, Lady Percy, urge him to
hold back from joining the rebels, though he feels his honour
demands it. His wife gives up her attempts to dissuade him –
'Do what you will, your wisdom be your guide' – but Lady
Percy has another, more challenging argument. Northumberland
forfeited his honour, she says, when he failed to join Hotspur's
troops at Shrewsbury,

> When your own Percy, when my heart's dear Harry,
> Threw many a northward look to see his father
> Bring up his powers; but he did long in vain.

Not only did he lose his honour, but Hotspur's too. In a rap-
turous evocation of the man she loved she torments his father
with her enumeration of his peerless qualities:

> He was indeed the glass
> Wherein the noble youth did dress themselves.
> He had no legs that practis'd not his gait;
> And speaking thick, which nature made his blemish,
> Became the accents of the valiant;
> For those that could speak low and tardily
> Would turn their own perfection to abuse,
> To seem like him. So that in speech, in gait,

In diet, in affections of delight,
In military rules, humours of blood,
He was the mark and glass, copy and book,
That fashion'd others. And him – O wondrous him!
O miracle of men! [she spares him nothing]
   – him did you leave –
Second to none, unseconded by you,
To look upon the hideous god of war
In disadvantage, to abide a field
Where nothing but the sound of Hotspur's name
Did seem defensible: so you left him.
Never, O never, do his ghost the wrong
To hold your honour more precise and nice
With others than with him! Let them alone.

This remarkable speech completes the portrait begun in
*Henry IV, Part I* of an exceptionally passionate and proud
marriage (perhaps the only one, I ventured to suggest in my
book on the earlier play, in the whole of Shakespeare). It also
brings before us again the unforgettable character paired
throughout the first play with Hal and finally slain by him, a
character synonymous with the chivalric ideal, which in
*Henry IV, Part II* is in effect dead. His resurrection (if only
verbal) serves again, as it did in the earlier play, to highlight
Hal's complexity by contrast with his own heroic simplicity;
but Hotspur is dead and Hal is alive, the simple hero van-
quished by the complex one. In the end, the effect of this is to
enhance our sense of the formidable nature of the man who
is to be king, though at this point in the play we can have no
clear guarantee of that outcome.

Northumberland is brought close to another emotional
breakdown, but knows: 'I must go and meet with danger there,
/ Or it will seek me in another place.' Lady Northumberland

urges him to go to Scotland to gauge the probable outcome before joining the rebels, and Lady Percy endorses this, again rubbing salt into her own and Northumberland's wounds, as she recalls how lack of foresight made her a widow. They are emotional people, these Northumbrians, strikingly more so than their southern counterparts. The ugliness and anguish of the scenes at Warkworth are powerful contributory factors in the darkening atmosphere of the play. By the end of the scene, Northumberland, deeply unhappy, ashamed of himself, makes a strong decision to remain firmly on the fence, and makes ready for Scotland.

## Scene iv: London. The Boar's Head Tavern in Eastcheap

We are, so to speak, backstage at the Boar's Head, and there is the usual drama: on this occasion, one of the drawers has laid on apple-johns, though Falstaff has a profound aversion to the withered old apples. It seems that Hal once abused Falstaff by comparing him to the same fruit, an insult somewhat lost on us, and indeed Falstaff himself has forgotten why he dislikes them so much; he simply does. Francis ('Anon! Anon, sir!') has the drawer cover them up, and then go to round up some musicians – Sneak's Noise, which would make a rather good name for a twenty-first century band; one can see the T-shirt – because Doll, who obviously has some weight in the establishment, has asked for music. Francis imparts the plot whereby Hal and Poins will pretend to be waiters, which strikes the kitchen staff as wildly funny: '. . . here will be old utis [as in carnival time]; it will be an excellent stratagem.' The servants scurry off to perform their various tasks, and Doll makes a brave if somewhat unsteady entrance, supported by Mistress Quickly, who has been plying her with sweet wine for strictly medicinal purposes. 'I'faith, sweetheart,' she reassures her in ever-inventive language, 'methinks now you are in an excellent good temperality.' At one point she says

> Your pulsidge [seeming to anticipate by 300 years Dickens's Mrs Gamp – *denied* the blessing of a daughter, and beholden to Mr Chuzzle*widge*] beats as extraordinarily as heart would desire, and your colour I warrant you is as red as any rose, in good truth, la! But i'faith you have drunk too much canaries, and that's a marvellous searching wine, and it perfumes the blood ere one can say, 'What's this?' How do you now?

Doll is better, though burping 'hem!', at which wholly fitting expression of bodily function, Sir John Falstaff appears with the noble utterance: 'Empty the jordan,' though whether he brings his own chamber pot in with him or whether he immediately detects the aroma from another's is unclear. In fact, he enters singing a misremembered line about King Arthur, and it seems quite right that this great pagan should be celebrating the Celtic Golden Age.

Gallantly he enquires after Doll; reassured by Mistress Quickly that her fever has subsided, Falstaff proceeds to a series of lewd references that result in a lively exchange with Doll herself:

DOLL A pox, damn you, you muddy rascal, is that all the comfort you give me?

FALSTAFF You make fat rascals, Mistress Doll.

DOLL I make them? Gluttony and diseases make them, I make them not.

FALSTAFF If the cook help to make the gluttony, you help to make the diseases Doll; we catch of you, Doll, we catch of you.

The tone declines, from sexual puns to violent abuse – 'you

29

muddy conger, hang yourself' – with substantial sexual over- and under-tones. Mistress Quickly is unfazed: 'By my troth, this is the old fashion; you two never meet but you fall to some discord.' Business is business, however, and she chides Doll as the weaker vessel, absent-mindedly adding that she is the emptier vessel – that is, one whose profession it is to be filled, is uncharacteristically empty. This provokes Doll to a more affectionate line of banter: 'Can a weak empty vessel bear such a huge full hogshead? There's a whole merchant's venture of Bordeaux stuff in him'; but she is in a mood for reconciliation, and even waxes tender towards him: 'Come, I'll be friends with thee, Jack, thou art going to the wars, and whether I shall ever see thee again or no there is nobody cares.' In a page, Shakespeare has sketched out an entire relationship based on deep physical and emotional intimacy – fierce and tender, coarse and caring, and fundamentally sexual. We are in the realm of the sonnets Shakespeare addressed to the Dark Lady, where idealization has no place, lust and respect being strangers, but where there is a profound knowing, a common realm of experience where nothing is mysterious, everything is lived-through. It is gratifying and messy and sometimes dis-gusting, but it has nothing to do with mental abstractions and all the destruction that the romantic heart can bring. It smells, and it belches, and it uses a piss-pot; it is real.

Into this momentarily relaxed atmosphere is unloosed Pistol, a wild cannon deeply unpopular with the female members of the establishment. Falstaff describes him as his 'Ancient' (just as Iago is Othello's ancient), but this seems, as Jorgenson says, 'a self-conferred honorific'. Doll knows him as a 'swaggering rascal . . . it is the foul-mouth'dst rogue in England.' Mistress Quickly is strongly opposed to swaggerers of every hue, and says so many times, as is her wont. She has been warned of 'swaggering companions' by no less a person than Deputy

Tisick (he must have a nasty cough) in the presence of the Reverend Dumb and enjoined to ban them from her premises, 'For . . . you are an honest woman.' Falstaff denies Pistol's swaggering tendencies: he is 'a tame cheater, i'faith, you may stroke him as gently as a puppy greyhound.' Mistress Quickly is trembling with anxiety by now: 'Feel, masters, how I shake, look you, I warrant you.' Doll confirms it. 'Do I?' says Mistress Quickly. 'Yea, in very truth I do, and 'twere an aspen leaf. I cannot abide swaggerers.' On cue comes Pistol, swaggering for England, punning madly on his own name, and approaching Doll with sexual innuendoes which are received with savage contempt. 'Away, you mouldy rogue, away! I am meat for your master.' There is something rather touching about this unglamorous assertion of Doll's relationship with Falstaff. She continues to berate Pistol with a fervour that seems to betoken some disgraceful past episode. She threatens to knife him, then pours scorn on his rank. 'Since when, I pray you, sir? God's light, with two points on your shoulder? Much!' Pistol responds with predictable volatility. In the mêlée, Falstaff tries to calm Pistol down, and Mistress Quickly makes the mistake of calling him Captain, which drives Doll into apoplectic rage, matched by Pistol's demand for revenge. First Bardolph and then the Page try to persuade him to leave, at which point he alarmingly transforms himself into a barnstorming thespian, howling blood-chilling curses from unknown plays at unseen adversaries, some of them canine:

To Pluto's damnèd lake, by this hand, to th'infernal deep, with Erebus and tortures vile also! Hold hook and line, say I! Down, down, dogs! Down, faitors! Have we not Hiren here?

At this point of histrionic hysteria he draws his sword, and anyone who has ever had to participate in a stage fight with an actor out of control will readily understand the panic that erupts on the stage at this point.

Each reacts differently. Mistress Quickly, perhaps struck by the priapic apparition of the drawn sword, rechristens him: 'Good Captain Peesel, be quiet, 'tis very late i'faith.' As always in trying circumstances, her vocabulary undergoes a nervous breakdown: 'I beseek you now, aggravate your choler.' But now Pistol has broken into verse, and there seems very little chance of him heeding her request, although his last line offers perhaps a tiny opening: 'Shall we fall foul for toys?' – that is, 'Shall we fall out over insignificant things?' After a few more rants, he suddenly becomes eirenic and lays down his sword with the stupendously enigmatic though no doubt sexually charged questions: 'Come we to full points here? And are etceteras nothings?' There is, understandably, no answer to that, except for an ominous growl from Falstaff: 'Pistol, I would be quiet'; but Pistol is still in full flight, and is overcome with a burst of affection for his leader: 'Sweet knight, I kiss thy neaf [fist]. What! we have seen the seven stars.' Doll is still hot for ejecting him, and after Pistol addresses another barb at her, Falstaff too has had enough: 'Quoit him down, Bardolph . . .' Pistol snatches up his sword and, equally alarmingly, lurches back into verse, which provokes Falstaff into snatching up his rapier and thrusting it at Pistol, who – no doubt stunned by the apparition of the fat knight roused to energetic action – flees.

The women immediately flutter around Falstaff. Mistress Quickly, who has been disturbed by the antagonists' 'naked weapons' – perhaps it is a professional deformation that everything turns sexual in her mouth – wants to know whether Falstaff has been hurt 'i' th' groin'. Doll tenderly assures him that 'the rascal's gone. Ah, you whoreson little valiant villain, you!' The scene now modulates, in the sort of transition that only Shakespeare and Chekhov seem able to manage, from the manic-depressive mayhem of the Pistol sequence into an episode of erotic tenderness and mutual fragility shot through with a kind of remembered bawdiness that is like chamber music. It is achieved by essentially musical means, Doll's cooing phrases like a mother's comfort, Falstaff her brave little chap who's fallen down and hurt himself, bragging as he dries his tears.

FALSTAFF A rascal, to brave me!
DOLL Ah, you sweet little rogue, you! Alas, poor ape, how thou sweat'st! Come, let me wipe thy face. Come on, you whoreson chops! Ah, rogue, i'faith, I love thee. Thou art as valorous as Hector of Troy, worth five of Agamemnon, and ten times better than the Nine Worthies. Ah, villain!
FALSTAFF A rascally slave! I will toss the rogue in a blanket.
DOLL Do, and thou dar'st for thy heart. And thou dost, I'll canvass thee between a pair of sheets.

Then, with his infallible theatrical instinct, Shakespeare adds instrumental music to the music of the words: Sneak's noise arrives and underscores one of the oddest and most affecting love duets, mingling love and death, in the whole of dramatic literature.

PAGE The music is come, sir.
FALSTAFF Let them play. Play, sirs! [*Music.*] Sit on my knee, Doll. A rascal bragging slave! The rogue fled from me like quicksilver.
DOLL I'faith, and thou followedst him like a church. Thou whoreson little tidy Bartholomew boar-pig, when wilt thou leave fighting a-days, and foining a-nights, and begin to patch up thine old body for heaven?

'Peace, good Doll,' he gently chides her, hearing the mortal note that has sounded from the beginning of the play and will sound over and over again, 'do not speak like a death's-head, do not bid me remember mine end.'

There follows an abrupt change in the scene, prompted by the stage direction: '*Enter*[, *behind*] *the* PRINCE *and* POINS *disguised* [*as drawers*].' Or is it? Doll suddenly questions Falstaff about Hal, which provokes him into his familiar flyting, randomly insulting both Hal and Poins, deriding the latter's alleged wittiness, and lumping them together as lightweight lads-about-town. Disguised and concealed, they are both outraged; Poins, with characteristic elegance, suggests beating him up in front of his whore. By now, however, Falstaff and Doll have turned to more interesting matters, resuming their hurdy-gurdy love duet. 'Is it not strange,' Poins memorably remarks, 'that desire should so many years outlive performance?' 'Kiss me, Doll,' says Falstaff, with uncommon simplicity, and when she does, he reproaches her: 'Thou dost give me flattering busses.' 'By my troth,' she says – and it is impossible not to believe her – 'I kiss thee with a most constant heart.' 'I am old, I am old.' 'I love thee better than I love e'er a scurvy young boy of them all.' Falstaff promises to buy her a skirt:

FALSTAFF  What stuff wilt have a kirtle of? I shall receive
    money a-Thursday, shalt have a cap tomorrow. A merry
    song! Come, it grows late, we'll to bed. Thou't forget me
    when I am gone.
DOLL  By my troth, thou't set me a-weeping and thou sayst so.
    Prove that ever I dress myself handsome till thy return . . .

Falstaff calls for sack, at which point the Prince and Poins reveal themselves.

Falstaff recovers himself well enough. First he calls Hal a bastard son of the King and Poins his brother; then, when challenged by Hal – 'what a life dost thou lead!' – he replies, wittily enough, 'A better than thou – I am a gentleman, thou art a drawer'; but he seems to have little interest in defending himself, squeezing Doll's 'light flesh and corrupt blood', and genuinely welcoming Hal in the most memorable of terms: 'Thou whoreson mad compound of majesty . . .' Doll is not best pleased by his description of her – 'You fat fool, I scorn you' – while Mistress Quickly arrives in radiant welcome of her most distinguished customer. It is like a homecoming, a family reunion, which displeases Poins no end – he had been hoping for a final reckoning with Falstaff: 'My lord, he will drive you out of your revenge and turn all to a merriment, if you take not the heat.' Hal does his best, accusing Falstaff of abusing him 'before this honest, virtuous, civil gentle-woman', a description that even Doll may find a little over-generous, though Quickly is delighted by it: 'God's blessing of your good heart! and so she is, by my troth.' Falstaff wants to know whether the Prince overheard him. Yes, says the Prince, and no doubt you're going to say, as you have in the past, that you knew I was there all along. No, says Falstaff, I didn't. So why did you abuse me? I didn't, says Falstaff. You didn't? says the Prince. No, says Falstaff, expertly ratcheting up the suspense:

> No abuse, Ned, i'th'world, honest Ned, none. I dispraised him before the wicked [*Turns to the Prince*] that the wicked might not fall in love with thee: in which doing, I have done the part of a careful friend and a true subject, and thy father is to give me thanks for it. No abuse, Hal; none, Ned, none; no, faith, boys, none.

It is one of Falstaff's greatest Houdini moments, his verbal escapology at its deftest. The Prince is having none of it, but Poins's worst fears have proved right: Hal has been completely sucked back into the Boar's Head world of games-playing, with its accusation and counter-accusation, its bluster and diversionary jokes, its warm and loving embrace of its own flaws. He functions, as he always has, as the perfect straight man to Falstaff's virtuoso comic improvisations. 'See now whether pure fear and entire cowardice doth not make thee wrong this virtuous gentlewoman to close with us,' says Hal, knowing full well how innocent in the conventional sense Doll is. 'Is she of the wicked? Is thine hostess here of the wicked? Or is thy boy of the wicked? Or honest Bardolph, whose zeal burns in his nose, of the wicked?' 'Answer, thou dead elm, answer,' says Poins, ever the Rottweiler, despite his master's affability. Falstaff picks his stooges off one by one in masterly melancholy style. 'What says your Grace?' asks Doll. 'His Grace says that which his flesh rebels against,' says Falstaff, with some profundity. There is a quibble in the phrase, contrasting grace and lust, but, more pointedly, it puts in a nutshell Hal's dilemma: the sensual self that must be subdued to the demands of kingship; it also seems to tell us that he has had sexual relations with Doll – in Dover Wilson's admirable exegesis: 'His "grace" (politeness) calls her a lady [gentlewoman] but his manhood knows her to be something very different.' That is how deeply Hal has entered into the life of Eastcheap.

There remains the question, not of great moment, but a tricky matter to be addressed in actual performance, of whether or not Falstaff knew that Poins and Hal were listening to the conversation. Doll's sudden change into questions about Hal immediately after they enter, and Falstaff's first sally against him – that he would have made a good pantler (pantryman), 'a would ha' chipped bread well' (that is, almost exactly the thing he is presently disguised as) – argues for him knowing; but the tender resumption of what I have called the love duet argues against it. It is also arguable that Falstaff's triumphant extrication of himself from the Prince's cross-examination is not prepared for in quite as masterly a fashion as I have suggested, and that Falstaff has simply had an inspired idea in the nick of time. Clearly, I have read the scene otherwise; I see no diminution of Falstaff's wit or any loss of self-regard, as others do. For me, the section of the scene in which Hal appears is a happy resumption of the glory days of their relationship, and it is so because Shakespeare is carefully preparing us for its terrible climax. Nor has Hal quite yet had his fill of what Falstaff and his cohorts give him: the sense of lived life, of play and of the primacy of instinct over intellect.

He is rudely precipitated into the other world, the world outside the womb that is the Boar's Head, with the arrival of Peto, who has surprisingly transformed into a figure from the world of action: in brisk blank verse, he introduces linearity into a scene that has up till now spread itself wherever it wanted to go.

> The King your father is at Westminster,
> And there are twenty weak and wearied posts
> Come from the north . . .

The actor has here to shine a cold, harsh light – a floodlight – into the muggy, diffused atmosphere into which he enters. It is not only Hal who is called to attention; Falstaff must snap out of his reverie too:

> . . . as I came along
> I met and overtook a dozen captains,
> Bareheaded, sweating, knocking at the taverns,
> And asking every one for Sir John Falstaff.

Hal doesn't need to be told twice.

> By heaven, Poins, I feel me much to blame,
> So idly to profane the precious time . . .
> Give me my sword and cloak.

He bids Falstaff good night. It is the last time they will meet until Hal is King, when everything is changed for ever.

Falstaff's response to the call to arms is unenthusiastic and somehow elegiac: 'Now comes in the sweetest morsel of the night, and we must hence and leave it unpicked.' Again, the key has changed, and with it the orchestration. Peto's trumpets and drums are replaced by bassoons, oboes, cellos, a meandering double-bass line padding through the scene – not without eruptions from outside, however. 'More knocking at the door?' asks Falstaff wearily. Bardolph tells him that no fewer than a dozen captains are waiting for him. He takes his leave, unexpectedly enjoining the Page to pay the musicians, and then making his farewells to the ladies: 'You see, my good wenches, how men of merit are sought after; the undeserver may sleep, when the man of action is called on.' He believes it – every word of it. 'Farewell, good wenches.' Doll and Quickly are both distraught, Doll close to tears: 'I cannot speak; if my heart be not ready to burst – Well, sweet Jack, have a care of thyself.' 'Farewell, farewell,' says Falstaff, and he's gone. The two women are left alone on the stage, bereft. The scene ends with a half-page of undiluted mastery – simple exchanges, monosyllables, mostly, broken phrases: a reminiscence, a tribute, a summons. Whole lives, entire relationships, human neediness, loss, love, all fill the stage, and these words, written four hundred years ago, reach us with exactly the same immediacy with which they reached Shakespeare's first audience.

HOSTESS  Well, fare thee well. I have known thee these twenty-nine years, come peascod-time, but an honester and truer-hearted man –Well, fare thee well.

BARDOLPH  [*At the door*] Mistress Tearsheet!

HOSTESS  What's the matter?

BARDOLPH  Bid Mistress Tearsheet come to my master.

HOSTESS  O, run Doll, run; run good Doll; come. She comes
   blubbered. [*To Doll*] Yea, will you come, Doll ?
*Exeunt.*

By the end of this overwhelming scene – structurally and to
some extent emotionally the equivalent of the first Boar's
Head scene in *Henry IV, Part I* – we know Falstaff in a very
different way from the way in which we have known him so
far. This is partly because he has changed – he is less limber
than he was, and he is conscious of his mortality – but mostly
because of the situations in which he is placed. His encounter
with the fantastical Pistol, a parody of a fighting hero, a sort of
clownish Hotspur, requires him to wield a sword and become
a sort of parody himself – of an outraged householder in
this case – after which he is treated with the sort of anxious
tenderness no soldier would expect or desire. His curious
ménage – Mistress Quickly wants to marry him, Doll attends
to his carnal needs – gives us something like a domestic
Falstaff, though here, as elsewhere, there is nothing merely
life-sized about him. The Boar's Head is his kingdom, where
he disports himself like a monarch, or a Bacchic god. By
some curious alchemy of the playwright, the exchanges, alternately tender and rebarbative, between an aged, obese, alco-
holic fallen aristocrat and his syphilitic doxy in a dubious pub
are neither squalid nor crudely comic: there is a sort of splendour about them, a majesty and a rightness that make them
curiously attractive. For all the frequently sounded dying fall
– not to mention the crazy firecracker of Pistol's eruption –
there is a mellowness, a fullness and an emotional freedom
about the scene that belongs to the carnival tradition of sat-
edness, of plenty and of celebration; the real location is not
Eastcheap in the city of London but the mythical land of
Cockaigne, the Middle Ages' dream of a place where, in the
words of its chronicler, Herman Pleij, 'roasted pigs toddle

about with knives in their backs to make carving easy; where grilled geese fly directly into one's open mouth; where cooked fish jump out of the water at one's feet. The weather is always temperate, the wine flows freely, sex is readily available, and all stay young for ever.'

It is part of Shakespeare's genius that what he writes is up to a point realistic, but that without compromising its credibility in any way he is able to inform it with the deeper resonances of the mythic. His evocation of the alternative kingdom renders its clash with, and its devastation by, the official kingdom all the more affecting. And the Falstaff we now follow into battle is a man of even more substance, in every sense of the word, than the one we thought we knew – not better, not nobler: he is still a liar, a cheat, a boaster, a slacker, a drunk; but he is something else too: a man who provokes love.

# Act Three

## Scene i: Westminster. The Palace

The King appears before us in his nightgown; he too is now revealed as a vulnerable human being. We know that he is ill; now we discover that he is also insomniac. Having despatched his Page to fetch the Earls of Surrey and Warwick, he launches into a moody meditation on sleep – or rather, on its elusiveness, a matter to which Shakespeare adverts so often in his plays and poems that it is difficult not to believe that he had some considerable personal experience of it. The King's theme here is that sleep is readily available to his subjects – even the humblest of them – but not to him: 'How many thousand of my poorest subjects / Are at this hour asleep!' He wonders how he has frightened sleep – 'nature's soft nurse' – and why sleep should choose to lie

in smoky cribs,
Upon uneasy pallets stretching thee,
And husht with buzzing night-flies to thy slumber,

when it eschews 'the perfum'd chambers of the great . . . lull'd with sound of sweetest melody'. His restless brain accuses the 'dull god' of turning the king's couch into the case of a watch, with its ever-turning wheels and its coiling and uncoiling springs, and to a stridently ringing alarm. Then his mental eye is filled with the image of a 'ship-boy', high in the rigging, sleeping peacefully through a violent storm. Elaborating on his notion of sleep as nature's nurse, he enviously sees it 'Seal up the ship-boy's eyes, and rock his brains / In cradle of the rude imperious surge', as the waves ride up 'With deafing clamour in the slippery clouds, / That with the hurly death itself awakes'. Bitterly he reproaches 'partial sleep' – partial in the sense of giving preference to the ship-boy over him – for denying him repose 'in the calmest and most stillest night'. 'Then happy low, lie down!' he concludes, fatalistically; 'Uneasy lies the head that wears a crown.' It is an aria such as Verdi or Mussorgsky might have composed. This king, like the king he usurped, is a poet, given to self-dramatization; unlike his predecessor, however, he is not a narcissist, and so, despite his travails, he is able to act, and act decisively, which now he proceeds to do.

The spectacle of the exhausted King is calculated to inspire pity and terror; it also gives a strong sense of the magnitude of what Hal is about to take on. Small wonder that he shies away from his destiny, or, to put it another way, that he needs to shore up his human resources before he takes it on. The King, for all his brilliance, his authority and his sense of responsibility, has in some important sense not been properly prepared for the task: it constantly threatens to overwhelm him. Whether this is due to the circumstances of his seizure of power (which he often seems to believe), or to some flaw in his own temperament (which is what his opponents believe), or whether, as I suggest, his assumption of power has not been part of a careful process of king-making, is part of the debate of the play – a crucial debate, because England's fortunes depend upon it.

The Earls enter in good cheer, but the King's mood remains melancholy, even despairing. Again he iterates the pervasive sense of physical decline that affects the land and all its inhabitants:

Then you perceive the body of our kingdom
How foul it is, what rank diseases grow,
And with what danger, near the heart of it.

Warwick is sanguine: 'good advice and little medicine' will effect a cure; but the King will not be so easily reassured. His despair goes beyond the immediate situation: it has its roots in history and fate; he broods on the mutability of human affairs, comparing them to nature's unending self-transformations:

> O God, that one might read the book of fate,
> And see the revolution of the times
> Make mountains level, and the continent,
> Weary of solid firmness, melt itself
> Into the sea, and other times to see
> The beachy girdle of the ocean
> Too wide for Neptune's hips; how chance's mocks
> And changes fill the cup of alteration
> With divers liquors!

What's the point? he asks.

> O, if this were seen,
> The happiest youth, viewing his progress through,
> What perils past, what crosses to ensue,
> Would shut the book and sit him down and die.

His own history haunts him: how Northumberland and Richard II were allies and friends, only to find themselves at war; how he and Northumberland became allies against Richard, who prophesied to Northumberland – 'thou ladder wherewithal / The mounting Bolingbroke ascends my throne' –

> The time shall not be many hours of age,
> More than it is, ere foul sin gathering head
> Shall break into corruption.

> (*King Richard II*, Act V, scene i)

And now, says the King, that time has come: '. . . this same time's condition / And the division of our amity'.

Warwick calmly points out that Richard's 'perfect guess' was based on a simple observation of the facts: Northumberland had betrayed Richard, so it was to be expected that he would betray Bolingbroke. 'Are these things then necessities?' cries the King, suddenly galvanized. 'Then let us meet them like necessities.' Warwick encourages him, doubting the rumoured numbers at Northumberland's disposal, and reporting the death of the ever-feared Glendower. Finally, consolingly, he reminds the King that he has been ill for a fortnight, that it is one o'clock in the morning, 'And these unseason'd hours perforce must add / Unto your sickness.' The King accepts Warwick's counsel, and concludes the session with an impassioned longing for his long-projected crusade to the Holy Land, instead of the present broils.

What is extraordinary in this remarkable scene is the emotional oscillation of the King, which is almost Slavic in its scope. It is not quite what we expect from a king, certainly not a soldier-king of Bolingbroke's colour. This apparent pragmatist, who constantly insists that he occupies the throne from no God-given right, much less from ambition – 'necessity so bow'd the state / That I and greatness were compell'd to kiss' – has inherited nothing but trouble. There has been no moment in his reign in which order and unity have prevailed; like Richard Nixon, he broods unceasingly on his destiny and the iniquity of his enemies. He is no villain, clearly, but, for a man of action, he is a disturbed, easily depressed individual, who needs at all times to be buoyed up by his associates. The contrast with Hal's substitute father, the reprobate Falstaff, could not be greater: the King turns everything to despair, while Falstaff turns commodity to advantage. Whose lessons are better for a future king?

### Scene ii: Gloucestershire. Before Justice Shallow's house

We are now taken to a world apart, having nothing in common with the King's Westminster or Falstaff's Eastcheap and blissfully ignorant of the bloody goings-on at the great battle-fields. There is some dispute among commentators as to where exactly we are – only later in the play is the location of Justice Shallow's house revealed as Gloucester, and it seems from certain allusions in the first Shallow scene that Shakespeare might have changed his mind halfway. In general terms, though, there is no question whatever where it is: the countryside, and, as ever, Shakespeare produces some of his most affectionate writing in evoking the sort of environment in which he grew up.

What we first see is an oddly assorted group: five working men of various shapes and sizes, a couple of servants, and two elderly gentlemen, one of whom is welcoming the other in easy and colloquial terms, with many repetitions, which we will come to know as highly characteristic of the speaker. 'Come on, come on, come on: give me your hand, sir, give me your hand, sir.' The man he addresses is called Silence, the speaker is Shallow; they are cousins. Silence is fittingly sparing of his utterances; Shallow has much to say about everything. There is family news to catch up on: '... how doth my cousin your bedfellow? and your fairest daughter and mine, my god-daughter Ellen?' 'Alas,' is the reply, 'a black woosel, cousin Shallow!' He is cursed with a brunette for a daughter, and in the 1590s, just as in the 1950s, gentlemen preferred blondes. The conversation continues along familiar domestic lines: how is the son; is he still at Oxford? 'Indeed, sir, to my cost,' replies Silence, again like any twenty-first-century middle-class parent. Shallow imagines that the son, William, will go on to the Inns of Court, to become a lawyer, which immediately precipitates him – it takes very little – into the land of memory. Like Mistress Quickly he has apparently total recall, effortlessly listing the names of all his contemporaries, although occasionally Silence – who has most certainly heard it all before, more than once – needs to correct him: 'I was once of Clement's Inn, where I think they will talk of mad Shallow yet.' 'You were called "lusty Shallow" then, cousin.' He is proud of his reputation as a ladies' man and a daredevil; sex is a fairly constant theme with him (as we might have guessed from his description of Silence's wife as his 'bedfellow'). He knew all the best whores, and had them at his fingertips. Among his companions was Falstaff, now Sir John, then 'a boy, and page to Thomas Mowbray, Duke of Norfolk'. It is only when Silence picks this up – 'This Sir John, cousin, that comes hither anon about soldiers?' – that we know why we are here at all, delightful though it is to encounter these elderly parties, one garrulity itself, the other the master of the one-liner.

Mention of Falstaff produces a burst of reminiscence; clearly the young Falstaff was quite a bruiser: 'I see him break Scoggin's head at the court gate, when a was a crack, not thus high . . .' Recollection of the past provokes a melancholy thought: 'And to see how many of my old acquaintance are dead!' Here it comes again, even in this bucolic idyll, the note of decline that tolls through the play. *Et in arcadia ego*. 'Death, as the Psalmist saith, is certain to all, all shall die.' But Justice Shallow being neither the head of state nor witness to the depredation of his own body, his melancholy mood is interspersed with questions of a more mundane order: 'How a good yoke of bullocks at Stamford fair?' and 'How a score of ewes now?'; but dead, dead, dead chimes through it all. Perhaps with some relief, Silence spots Bardolph, who identifies Shallow as a justice of the peace (as is Silence) and greets him from Falstaff. Shallow recalls Falstaff as a good fencer –

we're beginning to form quite a detailed impression of the young Falstaff – and enquires after his wife, an astonishing thought that Bardolph deflects by suggesting that 'a soldier is better accommodated than with a wife', a phrase that delights Shallow and leads to an unexpectedly learned philological disquisition by Bardolph. Shakespeare, whose grasp of his characters is absolute, constantly furnishes us with new aspects of them. A bookish and drink-sodden Bardolph makes perfect sense, as any denizen of the literary pubs of London will avouch.

Now Falstaff appears. Shallow finds him in good shape: 'By my troth, you like well, and bear your years very well,' which is probably nothing less than the truth, if we consider that – on the later evidence of this scene – he is at least seventy years old. Falstaff is all courtesy and social correctness, with a mild and pleasant joke on the name of the man he at first thinks is called Master Surecard. 'Good Master Silence, it well befits you should be of the peace.' It is hot, and Falstaff is eager to get on with things. His urgency pushes Shallow into a frenzy of repetitions: 'Where's the roll? Where's the roll? Where's the roll? Let me see, let me see, let me see. So, so, so, so, so, so, so.' He calls the men in turn for Falstaff's consideration. Falstaff is brisk, with a jest for each man, unable to resist puns on their names, easily done when they are called Mouldy, Shadow, Bullcalf and Wart. It is gallows humour for the most part; we know from *Henry IV, Part I* how high a price Falstaff sets on his soldiers' lives. Shakespeare, however, is incapable of creating mere cannon fodder, either for war or for Falstaff's wit: each man has a soul and a life. 'My old dame will be undone now for one to do her husbandry and her drudgery,' says Rafe Mouldy, on being selected. 'You need not have pricked me, there are other men fitter to go out than I.' Shadow is given less of a crack of the whip. 'Shadow will serve for summer. Prick him, for we have a number of shadows fill up the muster-book,' says Falstaff, frankly acknowledging that a lot of the recruits exist only on paper for the recruiting officer to claim his fee. Capriciously, Falstaff discounts Wart, apparently because his clothes are tattered; this strikes Shallow as the acme of wit. 'Ha, ha, ha! You can do it, sir, you can do it, I commend you well.' Bullcalf's desperate excuse that he has a cold, got ringing the church bells on the King's birthday, is brutally dismissed by Falstaff: 'Come, thou shalt go to the wars in a gown; we will have away thy cold, and I will take such order that thy friends will ring for thee' – funeral bells, no doubt.

The work thus briskly accomplished – this is a much reinvigorated Falstaff from the wheezing, addled, vulnerable figure whom we last saw reluctantly trudging off to war – Shallow invites him to dinner. Falstaff will drink with him, but not dine. Shallow plunges back into the past, a place to which Falstaff is by no means eager to follow him.

SHALLOW Oh, Sir John, do you remember since we lay all night in the Windmill in Saint George's Field?
FALSTAFF No more of that, good Master Shallow, no more of that.

But Shallow bounds further down the same path, fondly remembering the whores and brothels of yesteryear. It can only lead to one point: a recognition of age and mortality. 'Doth she hold her own well?' asks Shallow of one Jane Nightwork. 'Old, old, Master Shallow,' replies Falstaff, moodily. 'Nay, she must be old, she cannot choose but be old, certain she's old, and had Robin Nightwork by old Nightwork before I came to Clement's Inn.' Silence helpfully reminds the parties involved that it was fifty-five years ago (which is how we know that Falstaff is seventy or so). Shallow is not in the least dismayed by the statistic: it has been a full life and a merry one. 'Ha, cousin Silence, that thou hadst seen that that this knight and I have seen! Ha, Sir John, said I well?' Falstaff's recollection of that time is a chilly one: 'We have heard the chimes at midnight, Master Shallow.' 'That we have, that we have, that we have,' chortles Shallow, and ushers his guest and his cousin off for the promised drink.

Meanwhile the destinies of the recruits are at issue. Bullcalf and Mouldy bribe Bardolph with twenty and forty shillings respectively, which he accepts without argument. Feeble the tailor, a positive repository of popular phrases and sayings, proves surprisingly eager to fight.

By my troth I care not, a man can die but once, we owe God a death . . . No man's too good to serve's prince, and let it go which way it will, he that dies this year is quit for the next.

Falstaff, replenished, comes back; informed by Bardolph of the recruits who have bought themselves out, he swiftly deselects Mouldy and Bullcalf, to the mystification of Shallow. He then – perhaps this is the effect of the alcohol on his system – offers a magnificently perverse beginner's guide to successful recruiting.

Will you tell me, Master Shallow, how to choose a man? Care I for the limb, the thews, the stature, bulk, and big assemblance of a man? Give me the spirit, Master Shallow. Here's Wart; you see what a ragged appearance it is – a shall charge you, and discharge you, with the motion of a pewterer's hammer, come off and on swifter than he that gibbets on the brewer's bucket. And this same half-faced fellow Shadow; give me this man, he presents no mark to the enemy – the foeman may with as great aim level at the edge of a penknife. And for a retreat, how swiftly will this Feeble the woman's tailor run off! O, give me the spare men, and spare me the great ones.

He then has Bardolph thrust a musket into Wart's hands and takes him briskly through the drill, to his entire satisfaction, needless to say; he even rewards him with sixpence. Shallow is unconvinced, but immediately takes a sharp left turn down memory lane, recalling his days in amateur theatricals, where there was a fellow who . . .

Falstaff takes his leave. He has a dozen miles to cover tonight. Bardolph gives the soldiers their coats, and all depart, Shallow effusively cheering Falstaff on his way, with an urgent parting thought. 'At your return, visit our house, let our old acquaintance be renewed. Peradventure I will with ye to the court.' Falstaff is warm in reply: 'Fore God, I would you would, Master Shallow.' He obviously has a scheme in mind; and indeed, the moment the stage is empty, he tells us what it is. 'I will fetch off these justices. I do see the bottom of Justice Shallow.' Here he utters a curiously untypical phrase. 'Lord, Lord, how subject we old men are to this vice of lying.' This is the same Falstaff who only half an hour ago was telling the Lord Chief Justice: 'You that are old consider not the capacities of us that are young'; but then he was in adversarial mode. Now he is alone with us. Of course he will admit to being old; but admit to lying? Of course. We have seem him, in this play and the last, perform every kind of outrage. We are old friends. Now is the time for the truth. He brutally unmasks Shallow. 'This same starved justice hath done nothing but prate to me of the wildness of his youth, and the feats he hath done about Turnbull Street, and every third word a lie.' This is Falstaff the truth-teller, the realist, the man who says what no one else can dare to say: Falstaff the critic, the commentator, the balloon-pricker. 'When a was naked, he was for all the world like a forked radish, with a head fantastically carved upon it with a knife.' When did Falstaff see him naked? At the Windmill? Or side by side with Jane Nightwork? 'A was so forlorn, that his dimensions to any thick sight were invisible; a was the very genius of famine, yet lecherous as a monkey, and the whores called him mandrake.'

This is the once sturdy and well-built Falstaff, familiar of the great, dismissing the skinny little slip of a man:

> And now is this Vice's dagger [remember that in *Henry IV, Part I* Falstaff himself has been compared to the Vice of the medieval morality plays] become a squire, and talks as familiarly of John a Gaunt as if he had been sworn brother to him, and I'll be sworn a ne'er saw him but once in the tilt-yard, and then he burst his head for crowding among the marshal's men. I saw it and told John a Gaunt he beat his own name, for you might have thrust him and all his apparel into an eel-skin – the case of a treble hautboy was a mansion for him, a court;

'and now,' says Falstaff, with all the bitterness of those who have lived the incautious life, 'has he land and beefs. Well, I'll be acquainted with him if I return, and't shall go hard but I'll make him a philosopher's two stones to me.' He is natural prey for Falstaff. 'If the young dace be a bait for the old pike, I see no reason in the law of nature but I may snap at him: let time shape, and there an end.' This is not malice; it is simply the way of the world: predators predate.

It cannot be said that this scene makes us love Falstaff more. No doubt everyone can sympathize with the peculiar irritation inspired by an insignificant contemporary who ends up owning the factory. Falstaff has no truck with the past, and no desire to be reminded of it; but there is something a little brutal about the promised spectacle of seeing the amiable old justice gulled. Falstaff is not simply a deflater of pomposity, or an exploiter of stupidity, or a domestic tyrant in Eastcheap; he is a seasoned and determined con man. We like to think of Falstaff as being rather than doing – as surviving by various illicit means, but only in order to continue to be what he is, fully and without compromise. Here, though, we see that he can take a kind of professional interest in these survival tactics; the picaresque element comes more into focus. It is a new colour in a character whose dimensions – both physical and personal – seem almost limitless. This multifariousness is what led Anthony Quayle, a great post-war Falstaff, to assert that the character of the Fat Knight was richer, deeper and more fulfilling than that of King Lear, with which Quayle had also had a great success; Falstaff is inexhaustibly interesting, the manifestations of his being – despite his bodily decline – irrepressible.

# Act Four

### Scene i: Yorkshire. Within the Forest of Gaultree

While Falstaff greedily contemplates stripping Shallow of some of his wealth – having apparently forgotten the war in which he is about to participate – things are swiftly coming to a crisis in the martial world. The Archbishop and his party of rebels have come to rest in the royal forest of Gaultree, in Yorkshire, sending forth messengers to determine the numbers of the King's force. Meanwhile there is grim news in a letter from the Earl of Northumberland, regretting that the numbers he is able to muster not being consonant with his greatness, he has withdrawn to Scotland – as we knew he would. He concludes

> in hearty prayers
> That your attempts may overlive the hazard
> And fearful meeting of their opposite

– scant comfort from this serial absentee. A messenger arrives with the information that the enemy army has fielded 30,000: the exact number that the rebels expected. Mowbray urges them on.

Now Westmoreland appears as an emissary of the King's commander in the field, Prince John of Lancaster, and in measured, forceful tones reproaches the rebels – above all the cleric – for dignifying rebellion, 'guarded with rags, / And countenanc'd by boys and beggary', dressing its ugly form 'with your fair honours'. He asks of the Archbishop, with his learning and his piety, a man of God,

> Wherefore do you so ill translate yourself

Out of the speech of peace that bears such grace
Into the harsh and boist'rous tongue of war;
Turning your books to graves, your ink to blood,
Your pens to lances, and your tongue divine
To a loud trumpet and a point of war?

It is striking that in all their exchanges, rebels and establishment seek to claim the moral high ground; right as much as might is the issue.

In his response the Archbishop reiterates the very images with which the ailing King described the nation's state:

we are all diseas'd,
And with our surfeiting, and wanton hours,
Have brought ourselves into a burning fever,
And we must bleed for it; of which disease
Our late King Richard being infected died.

He claims not to see himself as a physician to this malady, but still finds himself pursuing medical metaphors:

But rather show awhile like fearful war
To diet rank minds sick of happiness,
And purge th'obstructions which begin to stop
Our very veins of life.

The kingdom, he seems to say, has fallen into hedonistic excess. Of this there is very little evidence in either part of *Henry IV*; and indeed, the Archbishop seems rather confused in his allegations (perhaps the result of a somewhat corrupt text at this point). Clarity is soon reached, however, when he complains that the King pays no attention to them:

When we are wrong'd, and would unfold our griefs,
We are denied access unto his person,
Even by those men that most have done us wrong.

Westmoreland flatly contradicts him: 'Whenever yet was your appeal denied? / Wherein have you been galled by the King?' The Archbishop insists that he speaks for 'the commonwealth'; again Westmoreland pooh-poohs him. Mowbray, perhaps rashly, adds his voice to the complaint, and Westmoreland, a dangerous man with whom to pick an argument, reminds him that when the King ascended the throne, he immediately restored Mowbray to all the lands and titles of his father, the former Duke of Norfolk.

This rouses Mowbray to a proud and passionate outburst that magnificently conveys the emotion that lies behind all of the rebels' complaints: they were all in it together, he insists, Bolingbroke simply one among equals within the chivalric order:

What thing, in honour, had my father lost,
That need to be reviv'd and breath'd in me?
The King that lov'd him, as the state stood then,
Was force perforce compell'd to banish him,
And then that Henry Bolingbroke and he,
Being mounted and both roused in their seats,
Their neighing coursers daring of the spur,
Their armed staves in charge, their beavers down,
Their eyes of fire sparkling through sights of steel,
And the loud trumpet blowing them together,
Then, then, when there was nothing could have stay'd
My father from the breast of Bolingbroke,
O, when the King did throw his warder down,
His own life hung upon the staff he threw;
Then threw he down himself and all their lives
That by indictment and by dint of sword
Have since miscarried under Bolingbroke.

This speech instantly makes real the rebels' cause. At such

moments (there are several throughout the play, and any play of Shakespeare's), the actor becomes the play's story-teller: he must seize the stage and make the picture he describes hang in the air before us as vividly and colourfully as any canvas in the National Gallery; he must become a film-maker, giving us wide shots and close-ups, tracking shots, background score and all. Time and again, these speeches are spoken by the supposedly less important characters; yet if they fail, the play is immeasurably reduced in its power and meaning. This is the democracy of Shakespeare's writing for a company of actors.

However thrilled the audience may be, Westmoreland, of course, is unimpressed: 'You speak, Lord Mowbray, now you know not what.' He slaps him down: Mowbray's father, he crisply tells him, was the most hated man in England; Hereford was the man people loved . 'But this is mere digression from my purpose.' Prince John, it appears, is in conciliatory mood. He will meet them

> and wherein
> It shall appear that your demands are just,
> You shall enjoy them, everything set off
> That might so much as think you enemies.

Mowbray is not appeased, and again articulates the rebels' deepest feelings: 'But he hath forc'd us to compel this offer, / And it proceeds from policy, not love.' Policy: the most despised word in the rebels' lexicon. They feel uncherished, and unequal, manipulated as part of some master plan. Westmoreland again ridicules their pretensions: the King's armies are overpoweringly superior in every department; they are under no political necessity. This offer proceeds from strength and should be greeted as such. Mowbray is suspicious; but Hastings and the Archbishop, once assured that Prince John has the full authority of his father, are swayed, and present their articles of grievance to Westmoreland, who promises to give them to 'the general', a curiously impersonal and somewhat threatening way of referring to the young Prince. Westmoreland is an ever more formidable figure, a political bully and grandee, not a Rottweiler, but a mastiff; the higher the status the actor is able to endow him with, the greater the King's power, and thus the higher the stakes for the play overall.

Left alone, the rebels are divided as to the merit of their decision. Mowbray fears the continued resentment of the King even if he pardons them; but the Archbishop believes that he now knows that his foes and friends are so close to each other that he can never wound one without harming the other. In a startling, unexpectedly domestic image – one reminiscent in language of Sonnet 143 –

> So run'st thou after that which flies from thee,
> Whilst I, thy babe, chase thee afar behind;
> But if thou catch thy hope, turn back to me,
> And play the mother's part, kiss me, be kind.

– he compares the state of England to that of a dysfunctional couple:

> So that this land, like an offensive wife
> That hath enrag'd him on to offer strokes,
> As he is striking, holds his infant up,
> And hangs resolv'd correction in the arm
> That was uprear'd to execution.

Hastings supports this view: the King, he says, has chastised so many that 'his power, like to a fangless lion / May offer, but not hold'. The Archbishop confidently expects that the forthcoming peace will 'like a broken limb united / Grow stronger for the breaking'; the play's central themes continue to find their expression in physical imagery.

**Scene ii: The same**

Scene ii is essentially a continuation, but its energy is transformed by the arrival of that chilly personage, Prince John of Lancaster, who, after a brisk general greeting, again denounces the hapless Archbishop in a sustained and scornful attack on the paradox of his position: a learned man, favoured by the King, God's spokesman, now become a man of war:

> My Lord of York, it better show'd with you
> When that your flock, assembled by the bell,
> Encircled you to hear with reverence
> Your exposition on the holy text
> Than now to see you here an iron man,
> Cheering a rout of rebels with your drum,
> Turning the word to sword, and life to death.

His privileged position of royal trust makes him doubly dangerous; while his position as God's spokesman, if abused, threatens the life of the nation. John speaks with icy contempt:

> Who hath not heard it spoken
> How deep you were within the books of God,
> To us the speaker in his parliament,
> To us th'imagin'd voice of God himself,
> The very opener and intelligencer
> Between the grace, the sanctities of heaven,
> And our dull workings? O, who shall believe
> But you misuse the reverence of your place,
> Employ the countenance and grace of heav'n
> As a false favourite doth his prince's name,
> In deeds dishonourable?

It is difficult to imagine a comparison more offensive to a priest – let alone a prelate – than to be likened to a monarch's minion, misbehaving under his master's protection. But John has more to say:

> You have ta'en up,
> Under the counterfeited zeal of God,
> The subjects of his substitute, my father,
> And both against the peace of heaven and him
> Have here up-swarm'd them.

'Counterfeited zeal' is a savage swipe, but more significant – anathema to the rebels – is the bald assertion that the King is God's *substitute*; the medieval order, here perishing on its feet, allows of no such substitution. God's servant, God's agent, perhaps; but God's substitute – never. Divine right in the monarch is something fiercely resisted by the baronial class, of whom, as we have seen, the King is simply the designated leader.

This speech of Prince John's brings a new tone into the play. He is the Robespierre of the Plantagenets, the ice-cold absolutist, all the more alarming for his youth. He begins to come into focus as a figure against whom we match Hal – so strangely absent for so long. What if John were the heir to the throne – he, whose sense of power and authority is unmediated by any experience of the life in which Hal has been immersing himself? It is a chilling prospect.

In the circumstances, York makes a restrained reply, disdaining to rise to any of the Prince's insults; he reiterates the rebels' resentment of the King's failure to respond to their complaints –

> The parcels and particulars of our grief,
> The which hath been with scorn shov'd from the court,
> Whereon this Hydra son of war is born

– but he holds out hope: its

    dangerous eyes may well be charm'd asleep
    With grant of our most just and right desires,
    And true obedience, of this madness cur'd,
    Stoop tamely to the foot of majesty.

So far, so conciliatory; but this is not submission. 'If not, we ready are to try our fortunes / To the last man,' Mowbray asserts. Hastings confirms this, and in a dire prediction threatens perpetual struggle unless their petitions are addressed: 'And heir from heir shall hold this quarrel up / Whiles England shall have generation' – a nightmarish prospect that echoes Northumberland's scorched-earth policy of the first scene of the play. Prince John hisses an insult to Hastings, which Westmoreland cuts short: how does his Highness like the articles of grievance? On this cue, John, in what appears to be a volte-face, turns brisk negotiator: he likes them all, allows them all, accepts that some of his father's supporters may have been a little overbearing. 'My lord, these griefs shall be with speed redresss'd; / Upon my soul they shall.' He enjoins them to dismiss their troops, as he will his:

    Let's drink together friendly and embrace,
    That all their eyes may bear those tokens home
    Of our restored love and amity.

The tone and simplicity of this speech are so different from anything that has so far passed the Prince's lips that it has the feel of a press release, an official communiqué; but neither York nor Hastings suspects anything, and they gladly give orders for the disbandment of their forces. Mowbray, significantly, is silent.

The Archbishop and Westmoreland, old colleagues, fall into easier discourse than we have so far heard, Westmoreland quietly pleased that the peace for which he has laboured seems imminent. Mowbray is suddenly taken ill, but he is gently ribbed both by the Archbishop and by Westmoreland, who affectionately addresses him as 'coz' – brother aristocrat. We hear the cheers of the men on hearing the news of peace – 'This had been cheerful after victory'; John gives orders for his army to stand down, and asks that the departing rebel soldiers march past as they quit the field. He trusts that 'we shall lie together tonight'. Hastings returns, memorably describing the dispersal of the rebel troops:

> Like youthful steers unyok'd they take their courses
> East, west, north, south; or, like a school broke up,
> Each hurries towards his home and sporting-place.

'Good tidings,' says Westmoreland,

> for the which
> I do arrest thee, traitor, of high treason;
> And you, Lord Archbishop, and you, Lord Mowbray,
> Of capital treason I attach you both.

The Archbishop gasps: 'Will you thus break your faith?' 'I pawn'd thee none,' says John.

> I promis'd you redress of these same grievances
> Whereof you did complain; which, by mine honour,
> I will perform with a most Christian care.

With a final slap in the face to the Archbishop, he says, as he leaves:

> God, and not we, hath safely fought today.
> Some guard these traitors to the block of death,
> Treason's true bed and yielder-up of breath.

This, one of the most naked episodes of *realpolitik* in all of dramatic literature, has inspired much commentary. Is John's action justified – or would it have been justified in the minds of the play's first audience – since it leads to the suspension of civil war, the worst affliction a nation can suffer? Certainly Hastings seems to promise a perpetuity of strife. Perhaps the only way to eliminate that possibility is by extirpating all rebellion; but we who live in an age of perpetual factional conflict – Israel–Palestine, Pakistan–India, USA–Al-Qaeda, Protestant–Catholic, Basque–Spanish – may find it hard to see things so simply. From a purely dramatic point of view, the scene is somewhat crude, even as Machiavellian manoeuvring, and it is my view that it is best considered as the ploy of a callous and callow young man, smart, bigoted, ruthless, devoid of humanity – in other words, as suggested above, a glimpse of exactly the kind of king England does not want.

### Scene iii: The same

The news of the departure of the rebel troops has not reached everyone. Falstaff now enters and bumps into another fighter who, on being amiably challenged, tells us that he is Sir John Colevile of the Dale; he recognizes Falstaff and, no doubt to Falstaff's surprise as much as ours, he sinks to his knees and surrenders. Falstaff meditates on his fame, which derives, he concludes, from his gut: '. . . my womb, my womb, my womb undoes me.' Prince John and Westmoreland return; Westmoreland is despatched to call the troops in. The Prince and Falstaff, with his prisoner, are left alone. Two opposite principles of the human condition confront each other. The Prince is immediately sharp with Falstaff – sharp, and then nasty:

When everything is ended, then you come.
These tardy tricks of yours will, on my life,
One time or other break some gallows' back.

Falstaff is uncowed by the Prince's hissing tone. He wants to play, like an oversized puppy encountering a polecat:

I would be sorry, my lord, but it should be thus. I never knew yet but rebuke and check was the reward of valour. Do you think me a swallow, an arrow, or a bullet? Have I in my poor and old motion the expedition of thought? I have speeded hither with the very extremest inch of possibility; I have foundered nine score and odd posts; and here, travel-tainted as I am [he adds, with wide-eyed wonder], have in my pure and immaculate valour taken Sir John Colevile of the Dale, a most furious knight and valorous enemy. But what of that? He saw me, and yielded; that I may justly say, with the hook-nosed fellow of Rome, three words, 'I came, saw, and overcame'.

The Prince is unamused by Falstaff's comparison of himself with the greatest general of antiquity, and snaps back, 'It was more of his courtesy than your deserving.' He is clearly uncertain how to deal with this odd creature, who then dumbfounds him by insisting that unless he, Falstaff, receives his due credit, he will have a ballad sung in honour of his heroic exploits – 'with mine own picture on the top on't, Colevile kissing my foot' – that will eclipse the Prince's achievements: 'I in the clear sky of fame [will] o'ershine you as much as the full moon doth the cinders of the element, which show like pins' heads to her ...' The world always seems a larger place when Falstaff speaks. Not of course to Prince John, who attempts to spar with Falstaff: 'Let desert mount,' says Falstaff. 'Thine's too heavy to mount,' comes the reply. 'Let it shine, then,' ripostes Falstaff. 'Thine's too thick to shine.' 'Let it do something, my good lord, that may do me good, and call it what you will.' Could Prince John ever be persuaded out to Eastcheap? Might he offer himself, one day, as Falstaff's pupil? Might he warm himself in Doll's lap? But he abandons his sparring match with Falstaff, and turns to Colevile, who, it transpires, is indeed a famous and a fierce rebel, who now claims that if his advice had been listened to, the cause might yet have prospered: 'Had they been rul'd by me, / You should have won them dearer than you have.' 'I know not how they sold themselves,' comments Falstaff pleasantly, 'but thou like a kind fellow gavest thyself away gratis, and I thank thee for thee.'

Westmoreland and soldiers return, and this episode, faintly unsettling to the tunnel-visioned young Prince, comes to an end in a flurry of commands, one of them to condemn Colevile to death. The King is gravely ill, the Prince reveals, and he is heading for the court. Falstaff has a request, delivered, uniquely for him in this play, in blank verse and with a rhyming couplet, his attempt, no doubt, at proper behaviour (he wants something, of course):

> My lord, I beseech you give me leave to go
> Through Gloucestershire, and when you come to court
> Stand my good lord, pray, in your good report.

The Prince, no doubt taken aback at this burst of metrical punctiliousness, replies: 'Fare you well, Falstaff. I, in my condition, / Shall better speak of you than you deserve.' But as soon as the Prince departs, the prose starts again: 'I would you had but the wit, 'twere better than your Dukedom.' He gives up on him: 'Good faith, this same young sober-blooded boy doth not love me, nor a man cannot make him laugh; but that's no marvel, he drinks no wine.' He develops this thought into a major theory of the beneficial effects of wine on human nature – in particular that sweet and admirably inebriating version of it, sherris-sack. Thin potions make men fall into a kind of male green-sickness; and then when they marry they get wenches. They are generally fools and cowards – which some of should be, too, but for inflammation.

His encomium of sack is developed into an aria of wonderfully sustained detail; all in all the speech would make a fine piece of advertising copy for the sherry industry:

It ascends me into the brain, dries me there all the foolish and dull and crudy vapours which environ it, makes it apprehensive [responsive], quick, forgetive [inventive], full of nimble, fiery, and delectable shapes, which delivered o'er to the voice, the tongue, which is the birth, becomes excellent wit.

Falstaff is, of course, the living proof of this.

The second property of your excellent sherris is the warming of the blood, which before, cold and settled, left the liver white and pale, which is the badge of pusillanimity and cowardice; but the sherris warms it, and makes it course from the inwards to the parts' extremes. It illumineth the face, which, as a beacon, gives warning to all the rest of this little kingdom, man, to arm; and then the vital commoners, and inland petty spirits, muster me all to their captain, the heart; who, great and puffed up with this retinue, doth any deed of courage; and this valour comes of sherris.

Inspired by this vision of a happily drunken world, his thoughts advert, as so often, to Hal, and he offers a sharp psychological insight into him:

Hereof comes it that Prince Harry is valiant; for the cold blood he did naturally inherit of his father he hath like lean, sterile, and bare land manured, husbanded, and tilled, with excellent endeavour of drinking good and good store of fertile sherris, that he is become very hot and valiant.

The dubious biology of this diagnosis notwithstanding, all the things associated with alcohol, most of them available on demand at the Boar's Head, have indeed transformed Hal – more, perhaps, than Falstaff realizes. Falstaff rounds off his commercial for sack with a rousing endorsement: 'If I had a thousand sons, the first human principle I would teach them should be to forswear thin potations, and to addict themselves to sack.'

Enter Bardolph, a living example of the effects of sack, who reports that the army is dispersed and gone. Falstaff sets forth for Gloucestershire. In a monstrous image, he tells us: 'I have him already tempering between my finger and my thumb, and shortly will I seal with him.' Poor Shallow, whom we have already been taught to see as a mandrake, a dace, and a radish, is about to become putty in Falstaff's fleshy paw.

### Scene iv: Westminster. The Jerusalem Chamber

The King, desperately ailing, is brought in on a chair: clearly he is failing. As so often, he is dreaming of a crusade to the Holy Land, 'if God doth give successful end / To this debate that bleedeth at our doors'. All he lacks is 'a little personal strength' and a reassurance that the rebels will finally be curbed. Warwick promises that it is only a matter of time, and the King turns to his sons Humphrey of Gloucester and Thomas of Clarence for news of Hal. Gloucester believes that he's hunting in Windsor – an extraordinary thought, since his younger brother John of Lancaster has until now been doing doughty battle in the field. Why was Thomas of Clarence not with him? Clarence steps forward to receive urgent advice from his father on how to handle Hal:

> . . . omit him not, blunt not his love,
> Nor lose the good advantage of his grace
> By seeming cold, or careless of his will . . .

The King proves to have studied his eldest son very carefully, and to have a lively sense of both his qualities and his defects:

> For he is gracious, if he be observ'd,
> He hath a tear for pity, and a hand
> Open as day for melting charity.
> Yet notwithstanding, being incens'd, he's flint,
> As humorous as winter, and as sudden
> As flaws congealed in the spring of day.
> His temper therefore must be well observ'd.
> Chide him for faults, and do it reverently,
> When you perceive his blood inclin'd to mirth;
> But being moody, give him time and scope,
> Till that his passions, like a whale on ground,
> Confound themselves with working.

The King's mind: always planning, weighing, assessing. He is concerned for Hal, for his brothers, for England:

> Learn this, Thomas,
> And thou shalt prove a shelter to thy friends,
> A hoop of gold to bind thy brothers in.

But why, the King wonders again, is Clarence not with Hal at Windsor? Because, the guileless boy replies, he is not there; he is in London, with Poins and his regular companions. This reply predictably shakes the father from his measured and balanced clarity into a state of morbid desolation, dreading what will happen to the kingdom:

Most subject is the fattest soil to weeds,
And he, the noble image of my youth,
Is overspread with them; therefore my grief
Stretches itself beyond the hour of death.
The blood weeps from my heart when I do shape
In forms imaginary th'unguided days
And rotten times that you shall look upon
When I am sleeping with my ancestors.
For when his headstrong riot hath no curb,
When rage and hot blood are his counsellors,
When means and lavish manners meet together,
O, with what wings shall his affections fly
Towards fronting peril and oppos'd decay!

Warwick, however, is less concerned:

My gracious lord, you look beyond him quite.
The Prince but studies his companions
Like a strange tongue, wherein, to gain the language,
'Tis needful that the most immodest word
Be look'd upon and learnt; which once attain'd,
Your Highness knows, comes to no further use
But to be known and hated.

Warwick, in other words, accepts the argument Hal advances in his first soliloquy, although we know that his feelings towards that world are far more interestingly and fruitfully complex than it would appear. The King is bitterly sceptical: ''Tis seldom when the bee doth leave her comb / In the dead carrion' – a dense and potent conjunction of images of the bee gorging itself on honey embedded in a rotten carcass.

The King's mood, though, is swept aside by messengers bringing ever better news: 'There is not now a rebel's sword unsheath'd / But Peace puts forth her olive everywhere.' No sooner does he hear these tidings than he succumbs to a violent spasm of his ailment, calling his sons to come near. Warwick urges them to stand off to give him air, and in fear they retreat into an urgent discussion; Clarence fears that 'he cannot long hold out these pangs. / Th'incessant care and labour of his mind,' he says, in a shocking image, 'Hath wrought the mure [prison] that should confine it in / So thin that life looks through and will break out.' His brother has heard reports of strange disturbances in nature, which Clarence matches. Both are certain that this is the end for the King; but then he comes round, asking to be taken to another room, in silence, unless someone 'will whisper music to my weary spirit'. They convey him to an upper part of the stage. Here, seamlessly, the next scene begins.

[Scene v]

The King has his crown laid on the pillow next to him; he sleeps.

At this point, Hal enters, briskly, certain that the King will have been revived by the good news from the front. Clarence urges them all to leave the sleeping King, but Hal insists on staying with him alone. Seeing the crown, he meditates on its terrible burden:

O polish'd perturbation! golden care!
That keep'st the ports of slumber open wide
To many a watchful night.

In terms that echo his father's words, he notes how light a king's sleep must be:

... not so sound, and half so deeply sweet,
As he whose brow with homely biggen bound
Snores out the watch of night.

But then his attention is caught by a detail:

> By his gates of breath
> There lies a downy feather which stirs not:
> Did he suspire, that light and weightless down
> Perforce must move. My gracious lord! My father!

This is the moment of truth for him – the moment that he has so long dreaded but to which every waking day has brought him a step closer: the death of his father, and the assumption of his father's crown. He takes it up.

> ... this is a sleep
> That from this golden rigol hath divorc'd
> So many English kings. Thy due from me
> Is tears and heavy sorrows of the blood,
> Which nature, love, and filial tenderness
> Shall, O dear father, pay thee plenteously.

But before that, overpowering that for the moment, is a sense of the massive responsibility that he now inherits:

> My due from thee is this imperial crown,
> Which, as immediate from thy place and blood,
> Derives itself to me.

He puts it on his head. His response is without ambivalence:

> Lo where it sits,
> Which God shall guard; and put the world's whole strength
> Into one giant arm, it shall not force
> This lineal honour from me. This from thee
> Will I to mine leave, as 'tis left to me.

He leaves the room. The King wakes up and finds the crown gone. In a panic, he summons his attendant lords.

This scene, which was almost a folk legend before

Shakespeare put it into his play (first appearing in the fifteenth century in Enguerrand de Monstret's *Chroniques*), provokes Shakespeare to write a scene of absolute theatrical mastery. Hal's cheerful entrance into the hushed chamber, his vigil at his father's bedside, the meditation on the crown that he has known from childhood must one day be his, the detail of the feather, Hal's hushed misapprehension that his father is dead, his tentative placing of the crown on his head – all of this is edge-of-the-seat stuff. Then his departure and the King's terror-stricken awakening: these are stage events that impress themselves on the mind for a lifetime.

'Warwick! Gloucester! Clarence!' The court rushes back to the King's chamber. The King wants to know why he has been left alone. They tell him that they left him with Hal. Where is Hal? Nobody knows. Where is the crown? He must have taken it. He sends Warwick to find him and reflects bitterly on Hal's greedy eagerness to seize the crown even before he, the King, is dead. 'See, sons, what things you are,' he unjustly accuses his two faithful children, 'How quickly nature falls into revolt / When gold becomes her object!' He thus falls into a long line of Shakespearean fathers ready to believe the worst of their children on the slenderest of evidence – Leonato in *Much Ado About Nothing* and Capulet in *Romeo and Juliet* come to mind. The King's ever-active brain elaborates this theme of thieving children with his characteristic rhetorical build-up, piling on the emotional effect:

> For this the foolish over-careful fathers
> Have broke their sleep with thoughts,
> Their brains with care, their bones with industry;
> For this they have engross'd and pil'd up
> The canker'd heaps of strange-achieved gold;
> For this ...

and so on. Finally he alights again on the image of the bee, but in a different sense from his comparison of Hal to a bee feeding on honey in a rotting carcass: this time he himself is the bee:

> When, like the bee, tolling from every flower
> The virtuous sweets,
> Our thighs pack'd with wax, our mouths with honey,
> We bring it to the hive; and like the bees
> Are murder'd for our pains. This bitter taste
> Yields his engrossments to the ending father.

The entomology is suspect, but the image crystal clear. Without breaking his stride, as Warwick returns he asks 'Now where is he that will not stay so long / Till his friend sickness have determin'd me?'

Warwick tells the King that he found Hal in an adjacent room, 'washing with kindly tears his gentle cheeks.' 'But wherefore did he take away the crown?' the King insists, querulously.

Now Hal enters the chamber and the King dismisses the court, leaving him alone with his heir for what promises to be a stormy interview. 'I never thought to hear you speak again,' says Hal, ashen. 'Thy wish was father, Harry, to that thought,' the King tartly retorts, in a peculiarly expressive phrase to preface an encounter that will be all about fathers and sons. The King starts with a tirade both sarcastic and deeply wounded, of which the governing idea is stated in the opening salvo: 'I stay too long by thee, I weary thee.' But why is Hal so impatient?

> Stay but a little, for my cloud of dignity
> Is held from falling with so weak a wind
> That it will quickly drop; my day is dim.

Hal never loved him, and he wants him to die knowing it.

> Thou hid'st a thousand daggers in thy thoughts,
> Which thou hast whetted on thy stony heart,
> To stab at half an hour of my life.
> What, canst thou not forbear me half an hour?

We know that this is not how the King sees Hal – he knows that he is, as he has just told Thomas of Clarence, kind-hearted and generous; but the death-bed is no place for cool reason when the fate of England is at stake.

In expertly placed blow after blow, he batters Hal with wild reproaches in some of which there may be a grain of truth, but all of which are designed to sweep away any inhibition from the confrontation: by its end, they must have said everything to each other. There will be no second chance. The grave yawns.

> Then get thee gone, and dig my grave thyself,
> And bid the merry bells ring to thine ear
> That thou art crowned, not that I am dead.
> Let all the tears that should bedew my hearse
> Be drops of balm to sanctify thy head,
> Only compound me with forgotten dust.
> Give that which gave thee life unto the worms.

Here he uses the language of the sonnets, in the context of an altogether different relationship, but one where the speaker is equally haunted by a sense of his own failure to provoke love:

> No longer mourn for me when I am dead
> Than you shall hear the surly sullen bell
> Give warning to the world that I am fled
> From this vile world with vilest worms to dwell.
>
> (Sonnet 71)

He foresees not only his unregarded death but the death of everything he strove for:

Pluck down my officers; break my decrees;
For now a time is come to mock at form –
Harry the fifth is crown'd!

Then he paints a nightmare picture of the reign to come, that of Henry V:

Up, vanity!
Down, royal state! All you sage counsellors, hence!
And to the English court assemble now
From every region, apes of idleness!
Now, neighbour confines, purge you of your scum!
Have you a ruffian that will swear, drink, dance,
Revel the night, rob, murder, and commit
The oldest sins the newest kind of ways?

Anarchy will engulf the realm.

For the fifth Harry from curb'd licence plucks
The muzzle of restraint, and the wild dog
Shall flesh his tooth on every innocent.
O my poor kingdom, sick with civil blows!
When that my care could not withhold thy riots,
What wilt thou do when riot is thy care?
O, thou wilt be a wilderness again,
Peopled with wolves, thy old inhabitants!

If the purpose of all this is to make Hal weep, it succeeds almost too well: he has been unable to speak for tears, 'the moist impediments unto [his] speech'. Begging the King's pardon, he restores the crown to him, praying 'And He that wears the crown immortally / Long guard it yours!' He describes his actions when he thought his father was dead: 'How cold it struck my heart!' He reproached the crown thus, he says:

... thou best of gold art worst of gold.
Other, less fine in carat, is more precious,
Preserving life in med'cine potable;
But thou, most fine, most honour'd, most renown'd,
Hast eat thy bearer up.

He put it on his own head, 'To try with it, as with an enemy /
That had before my face murder'd my father.' If he felt one
surge of pleasure, one second of delight on wearing it, he
protests,

Let God for ever keep it from my head,
And make me as the poorest vassal is,
That doth with awe and terror kneel to it!

This passionate speech, too, finds its mark:

O my son,
God put it in thy mind to take it hence,
That thou mightst win the more thy father's love,
Pleading so wisely in excuse of it!

Neither can doubt the intensity of the other's feeling, or the
depth of love on both sides. The King, practical as ever despite
the emotional flights to which he is prone, gives his final
urgent advice to the son who is so shortly to ascend the
throne; his strength is ebbing away before Hal's eyes:

Come hither, Harry, sit thou by my bed,
And hear, I think, the very latest counsel
That ever I shall breathe.

First, he rehearses again the reasons for the troubles of his
reign:

God knows, my son,
By what by-paths and indirect crook'd ways

I met this crown, and I myself know well
How troublesome it sat upon my head.

For Hal it will be different: '. . . the soil' [that is, the dirt] 'of the
achievement goes / With me into the earth.' There were too
many people who had helped him to the throne who could
never see him as the legitimate King:

> It seem'd in me
> But as an honour snatch'd with boist'rous hand,
> And I had many living to upbraid
> My gain of it by their assistances,
> Which daily grew to quarrel and to bloodshed,
> Wounding supposed peace.

In a vivid theatrical image, he expresses the exhaustion and
the pointlessness of what followed: 'For all my reign hath been
but as a scene / Acting that argument' – play-acting, he
implies.

It will be easier for Hal, who is evidently the legitimate suc-
cessor; but with chilling realism he teaches Hal to beware the
King's associates:

> all my friends, which thou must make thy friends,
> Have but their stings and teeth newly ta'en out;
> By whose fell working I was first advanc'd,
> And by whose power I well might lodge a fear
> To be again displac'd.

He had a stratagem in place to distract them:

> I cut them off, and had a purpose now
> To lead out many to the Holy Land,
> Lest rest and lying still might make them look
> Too near unto my state.

For all the scholarly discussions of the legitimacy of this ploy by the standards of Elizabethan statecraft, it is impossible not to be chilled by the naked cynicism of it; the King, in extremis, does not even attempt to justify it with religious sentiment. Here the barons' contempt for the King's 'policy' – Hotspur repeatedly jibes in *Henry IV, Part I* against 'this *politician* Bolingbroke' – seems entirely apt. No less chilling to a modern audience is the King's last word of advice to his son:

> Therefore, my Harry,
> Be it thy course to busy giddy minds
> With foreign quarrels, that action hence borne out
> May waste the memory of the former days.

This, of course, is the action of *Henry V*, where the Machiavellian inspiration of the war is underplayed.

After the extraordinary emotional intensity of the King's first speech to Hal, and Hal's response, this swift descent into calculation and manipulation is shocking but entirely realistic, and much of the matter of successful kingship. Hal's lessons, which have scarcely stopped since the second scene of *Henry IV, Part I*, are coming to an end. Between the Academies of Eastcheap and Westminster, with practical applications on the Field of Battle, they have covered many aspects of what it is to be a son, what it is to be a King, and what it is to be a man. The moment of Hal's translation into a monarch is imminent. 'More would I,' says the King,

> but my lungs are wasted so
> That strength of speech is utterly denied me.
> How I came by the crown, O God forgive,
> And grant it may with thee in true peace live!

Hal faces his coming responsibility with strength and confidence, and with resounding rhymes – always a sign of something coming to an end in Shakespeare:

> My gracious liege,
> You won it, wore it, kept it, gave it me;
> Then plain and right must my possession be,
> Which I with more than with a common pain
> 'Gainst all the world will rightfully maintain.

The court returns, among them the victorious John of Lancaster, who rouses the King to great affection: to the young Prince's greeting of 'Health, peace, and happiness to my royal father!' he replies,

> Thou bring'st me happiness and peace, son John,
> But health, alack, with youthful wings is flown
> From this bare wither'd trunk. Upon thy sight
> My worldly business makes a period.

He is barely alive now. He discovers from Warwick that the room in which he fainted earlier in the scene is the Jerusalem Chamber.

> Laud be to God! Even there my life must end.
> It hath been prophesied to me, many years,
> I should not die but in Jerusalem,
> Which vainly I suppos'd the Holy Land.
> But bear me to that chamber; there I'll lie;
> In that Jerusalem shall Harry die.

The scene, and the life of King Henry IV, ends with a profound sense of rightness.

# Act Five

### Scene i: Gloucestershire. Shallow's house

We find ourselves back in Gloucestershire, which, after the epic activities of the previous scene, seems at first to belong not merely to another world but to another play. It takes a little time to adjust to Shallow's conversational loops: when Falstaff cries off dinner, the garrulous justice cries, as if conjugating the verb *excuse*, 'I will not excuse you, you shall not be excused, excuses shall not be admitted, there is no excuse shall serve, you shall not be excused.' He calls for his servant Davy, and addresses him with the repetitiveness of someone treading verbal water till his thoughts are clarified: 'Davy, Davy, Davy, Davy; let me see, Davy; let me see, Davy; let me see – yea, marry, William cook, bid him come hither.' Having produced the magnificent new thought about the cook like a magician producing a rabbit from a hat, he returns to an earlier success. 'Sir John, you shall not be excused.' Life, to Falstaff's impatience, goes on around him at exactly the speed and with as much attention to the mundane as it always does. There are questions about the sowing of seeds, about possible pigeon for supper, about the problem with the bucket, about paying for the shoeing and plough-irons, about the lost sack. 'Sir John, you shall not be excused.' A decision is made about dinner – and a very good one it sounds – 'Some pigeons, Davy, a couple of short-legged hens, a joint of mutton, and any pretty little kickshaws [amuse-gueules], tell William cook.' Davy asks whether the 'man of war' will stay all night. Yes, says Shallow, 'I will use him well: a friend i'th'court is

79

better than a penny in purse.' So Shallow is quite as crafty as Falstaff: who is exploiting whom? Shallow tells Davy to use Falstaff's retinue well, too, 'for they are arrant knaves and will back-bite'. 'No worse than they are back-bitten, sir,' replies the witty servant, 'for they have marvellous foul linen,' which makes Shallow laugh. Then Davy puts in a word for his friend Visor, a self-confessed knave,

> but yet God forbid, sir, but a knave should have some countenance at his friend's request. An honest man, sir, is able to speak for himself, when a knave is not. I have served your worship truly, sir, this eight years; and if I cannot once or twice in a quarter bear out a knave against an honest man, I have but a very little credit with your worship. The knave is mine honest friend, sir, therefore I beseech your worship let him be countenanced.

Faced with this masterly piece of candour (which would not be out of place in the mouth of Shaw's Alfred Doolittle), of course Shallow will be persuaded. 'Go to; I say he shall have no wrong.'

Within three pages Shakespeare has taken us to a world unimaginable to the denizens of Westminster (though not, of course, to Hal): a world of petty concerns, of sensual satisfaction, of easy social relations, of no fixed moral absolutes. The terrible stark blacks and whites, the rigid hierarchies, the bull-headed certainties of Henry IV's court are inconceivable here. Shakespeare evokes those realities in majestic and sometimes tortured blank verse, full of soaring images, complex metaphors and grand ideas; they seem to have been written in steel or shot silk. This bucolic world, by deep contrast, is a kind of home weave of banalities, sly jokes, concrete nouns and repeated catchphrases. Falstaff regards it with appalled fascination. After being persuaded to take his boots off, and after his little court of Bardolph and the Page have been warmly greeted, he is left alone and shares his observations with us. They are particularly acute, almost analytical, and hit the nail bang on the head:

> It is a wonderful thing to see the semblable coherence of his men's spirits and his. They, by observing of him, do bear themselves like foolish justices; he, by conversing with them, is turned into a justice-like servingman. Their spirits are so married in conjunction, with the participation of society, that they flock together in consent, like so many wild geese.

Quite apart from the sharpness of his brain, of which we have plentiful evidence already, this tells us something new about Falstaff: he is a great observer. He is certainly not one of those 'characters' whose only subject is himself; he watches, he listens, and he learns.

There is another point, too: it provides him very good material for his comedy:

> I will devise matter enough out of this Shallow to keep Prince Harry in continual laughter the wearing out of six fashions, which is four terms, or two actions, and a shall laugh without intervallums. O, it is much that a lie with a slight oath, and a jest with a sad brow, will do with a fellow that never had the ache in his shoulders! O, you shall see him laugh till his face be like a wet cloak ill laid up!

We, who have witnessed Hal's most recent rites of passage, may wonder whether Falstaff has not, at last, misjudged his royal audience; but meanwhile there is supper – that excellent supper – to be had. 'Sir John!' 'I come, Master Shallow, I come, Master Shallow.' The circular conversational method is evidently catching.

## Scene ii: Westminster. The palace

A million miles away, in Westminster, news of the King's death is only just spreading, and with it, fear for the future. The Lord Chief Justice hastens in; on hearing from the Earl of Warwick that the King has 'walk'd the way of nature, / And to our purposes he lives no more', he immediately becomes anxious for himself. 'Indeed,' Warwick bluntly informs him, 'I think the young King loves you not.' The Lord Chief Justice is well aware of the extreme danger of his position: he has armed himself, he says,

> To welcome the condition of the time,
> Which cannot look more hideously upon me
> Than I have drawn it in my fantasy.

This deep anxiety is, it appears, universal: even Warwick, who defended Hal to his father, shares it. On seeing Hal's three brothers, he fervently wishes that one of them might have been the heir: 'How many nobles then should hold their places / That must strike sail to spirits of vile sort.' A tense and doleful conversation ensues: 'We meet like men that had forgot to speak.' Clarence crisply articulates the Lord Chief Justice's worst nightmare: 'Well, you must now speak Sir John Falstaff fair.' The lawman is unrepentant, ready to die rather than compromise his devotion to the law: 'I'll to the King my master that is dead, / And tell him who hath sent me after him.' At which point, *Enter King Henry V, attended*, as the stage direction tells us. 'Good morrow, and God save your Majesty!' cries the Lord Chief Justice. Whatever he might have expected is confounded by the new King's first utterance, which is modest, human, reflective: 'This new and gorgeous garment, majesty, / Sits not so easy on me as you think.' Sensing the tension, he addresses his brothers:

... you mix your sadness with some fear.
This is the English, not the Turkish court;
Not Amurath an Amurath succeeds,
But Harry Harry.

His choice of words is unerring – not 'Henry', but 'Harry'.

Yet be sad, good brothers,
For by my faith it very well becomes you.
Sorrow so royally in you appears
That I will deeply put the fashion on,
And wear it in my heart. Why then, be sad,

he says; and then, with masterly inclusiveness, he stresses
their solidarity:

But entertain no more of it, good brothers,
Than a joint burden laid upon us all.
For me, by heaven, I bid you be assur'd,
I'll be your father and your brother too;
Let me but bear your love, I'll bear your cares.

No doubt a little nonplussed at this unaccustomed maturity from the wildcat older brother, the Princes blurt out
together: 'We hope no otherwise from your Majesty'; but the
anxiety is still not fully dispersed. 'You all look strangely on
me,' the new King notes, 'and you most,' he says to the Lord
Chief Justice. 'You are, I think, assur'd I love you not.'

Carefully, the lawman replies that the new King has no
cause to hate him; and now Hal replies in a tone that tells us
that he has not exchanged one personality for another – this
is recognizably the Hal of the Boar's Head, dangerously play-
ful, affecting an anger that he partly feels: 'No?' It is a one-syl-
lable line, leaving the unspoken nine syllables hanging
ominously in the air.

> How might a prince of my great hopes forget
> So great indignities you laid upon me?
> What! Rate, rebuke, and roughly send to prison
> Th'immediate heir of England? Was this easy?
> May this be wash'd in Lethe and forgotten?

Staunchly the Lord Chief Justice defends himself: it was not he but his office, 'The majesty and power of law and justice, / The image of the King whom [he] presented', that was struck when Hal boxed his ears. How would you like it, he asks Hal, if your son were to do the same to me, now you are King? He invites him to dramatize the situation, an approach calculated to appeal to one who has shown himself to have a singular capacity to learn from acting things out:

> Question your royal thoughts, make the case yours,
> Be now the father, and propose a son,
> Hear your own dignity so much profan'd,
> See your most dreadful laws so loosely slighted,
> Behold yourself so by a son disdain'd:
> And then imagine me taking your part,
> And in your power soft silencing your son.
> After this cold considerance sentence me;
> And, as you are a king, speak in your state
> What I have done that misbecame my place,
> My person, or my liege's sovereignty.

Hal is well pleased with this, but his magnanimity far exceeds what even the Lord Chief Justice might have hoped for. Personifying him as the very principle that he defends, he tells him:

> You are right, Justice, and you weigh this well.
> Therefore still bear the balance and the sword;

And I do wish your honours may increase
Till you do live to see a son of mine
Offend you and obey you, as I did.

He urges him to use the symbolic sword of justice 'With the
like bold, just, and impartial spirit / As you have done 'gainst
me,' and concludes:

There is my hand.
You shall be as a father to my youth,
My voice shall sound as you do prompt mine ear,
And I will stoop and humble my intents
To your well-practis'd wise directions.

Now he addresses his brothers: 'My father is gone wild into
his grave, / For in his tomb lie my affections' – the dead King
has taken Hal's wildness with him to the tomb –

And with his spirits sadly I survive
To mock the expectation of the world,
To frustrate prophecies, and to raze out
Rotten opinion, who hath writ me down
After my seeming.

Changing the focus from past to future, he continues:

The tide of blood in me,
Hath proudly flow'd in vanity till now.
Now doth it turn, and ebb back to the sea,
Where it shall mingle with the state of floods,
And flow henceforth in formal majesty.

As he speaks, he becomes a king. The energy and force of his
utterance grow with every line, till we hear the characteristic
tone of the Henry V with whom we are so familiar from the
play that bears his name.

The speech is a transformation scene in itself, as the tentative, newly wise ruler reconciles those he has alienated, lays plans for his rule, and finally, thrillingly, becomes the voice of England. Trumpets and timpani sound out; it is a musical passage of exceptional excitement as a united nation shining with hope and new life seems to emerge from the murky past.

> Now call we our high court of parliament,
> And let us choose such limbs of noble counsel
> That the great body of our state may go
> In equal rank with the best-govern'd nation;
> That war, or peace, or both at once, may be
> As things acquainted and familiar to us;
> In which you, father, shall have foremost hand.
> Our coronation done, we will accite [summon],
> As I before remember'd, all our state:
> And, God consigning to my good intents,
> No prince nor peer shall have just cause to say,
> God shorten Harry's happy life one day!

### Scene iii: Gloucestershire. Shallow's orchard

As things become clearer and brighter at the centre of power, back in Gloucestershire things are going very soft round the edges. Shallow is boasting of his orchard and promising apples bred by him; Falstaff can only admire and envy. Shallow's needle is stuck again: 'Barren, barren, barren; beggars all, beggars all, Sir John.' He admits the air is good and then calls Davy: 'Spread, Davy, spread, Davy, well said, Davy.' Falstaff expresses his admiration for Davy, both steward and serving-man. 'A good varlet, a good varlet, a very good varlet, Sir John – by the mass, I have drunk too much sack at a supper – a good varlet.' Silence, meanwhile, has found his voice, and starts to sing, with some spirit. Falstaff urges him on. Davy is being a good host, topping up Bardolph's glass and that of the Page. Falstaff continues to be amazed at Silence's party spirit. 'Who, I? I have been merry twice and once ere now.' Davy distributes apples, Silence sings, Shallow toasts Bardolph and the Page, Davy dreams of going to London; nothing happens. The Prozorovs, or Uncle Vanya and Sonia, would be perfectly at home here, but for the want of a samovar. Loud knocking cuts through the woozy texture. Silence, having astonished Falstaff by matching him glass for glass, sings saucy Spanish songs, while Davy answers the door. It's Pistol.

Immediately Falstaff snaps out of the prevailing drowsiness: 'From the court? Let him come in.' 'Sweet knight,' Pistol tells him, 'thou art now one of the greatest men in the realm.' Silence makes a fatuous joke about Falstaff's avoirdupois, which Pistol answers viciously. He continues to give his news, but he is now in full histrionic mode, and it takes some ingenuity to extract his meaning from him:

And helter-skelter have I rode to thee,
And tidings do I bring, and lucky joys,
And golden times, and happy news of price.

'I pray thee now,' says Falstaff, 'deliver them like a man of this world.' 'A foutre for the world and worldlings base! / I speak of Africa and golden joys.' Falstaff gamely tries to join in: 'O base Assyrian knight, what is thy news? / Let King Cophetua know the truth thereof.' Silence adds his two-penn'orth: '[*Sings*] And Robin Hood, Scarlet, and John,' which inspires Pistol to wilder flights:

Shall dunghill curs confront the Helicons?
And shall good news be baffled?
Then, Pistol, lay thy head in Furies' lap.

The dramatist's audacity at this point is breathtaking, leaving the other characters onstage gagging for information that we, the audience, already know. Things continue in this Alice-in-Wonderland mode, with Silence contrapuntally interpolating inebriated irrelevancies, until Shallow can bear it no more, and the truth slips out: 'Give me pardon, sir; if, sir, you come with news from the court,' he says, giving us a glimpse of his courtroom manner, 'I take it there's but two ways, either to utter them or conceal them. I am, sir, under the King, in some authority.' Pistol does not buckle under cross-examination: 'Under which king, Besonian?' He is calling Shallow a know-nothing, *un bisogno*, lacking in grey matter. 'Speak, or die.' 'Under King Harry,' says Shallow. 'Harry the Fourth, or Fifth?' 'Harry the Fourth.' 'A foutre for thine office!' cries the triumphant Pistol, casting Shallow aside:

> Sir John, thy tender lambkin now is King;
> Harry the Fifth's the man: I speak the truth.
> When Pistol lies, do this, and fig me, like
> The bragging Spaniard.

Falstaff is momentarily numbed: 'What, is the old King dead?' The moment he has confirmation, he is off like a greyhound out of a trap, celebrating his new power:

> Away, Bardolph, saddle my horse. Master Robert Shallow, choose what office thou wilt in the land, 'tis thine. Pistol, I will double-charge thee with dignities.

Bardolph declines a knighthood as Falstaff's imagination begins to work: 'Master Shallow, my Lord Shallow – be what thou wilt; I am Fortune's steward!' Silence meanwhile has fallen asleep. Falstaff sweeps Shallow up with him. 'Get on thy boots, we'll ride all night.' 'O sweet Pistol!' cries Falstaff. 'Utter more to me; and withal devise something to do thyself good. Boot, boot,

Master Shallow!' His grandiose vision of how he as Fortune's steward will proceed is mingled with anticipated delight at his reception when he is reunited with Hal: 'I know the young King is sick for me.' The Lord Chief Justice's worst fears are amply confirmed, both with regard to the law in general and to himself in particular: 'Let us take any man's horses – the laws of England are at my commandment. Blessed are they that have been my friends, and woe to my Lord Chief Justice!' Pistol, of course, has to bring the curtain down on the scene:

> Let vultures vile seize on his lungs also!
> 'Where is the life that late I led?' say they:
> Why, here it is; welcome these pleasant days.

The scene with its soporific, motiveless first half and its electrifying second, boots and saddles flying in all directions, manic Pistol verbally shooting from the hip, one elderly justice of the peace passing out, another desperately trying to keep pace, and Falstaff in triumph, roused to monstrous energy, is a tour de force of dramatic writing, but it is something more than that because of the scene that precedes it. We know that Falstaff's hopes and aspirations – whatever we may think of them – are doomed. This has the effect of rendering him both harmless (in terms of his disgraceful plans for advancing his friends) and touching, since we have seen his enemies honoured and his patron transformed so completely that Falstaff could never have any future place in his life. The mixture of emotions thus created in us as we watch is typical of the complexity of Shakespeare's art: we disapprove of Falstaff, but we are touched by him; we approve of Hal's ascent to maturity and kingship, and we know that he must discard Falstaff but can hardly bear the prospect of his being rejected. The play hurtles towards exactly that, and we are taken with it; but the temptation to avert our eyes is strong.

### Scene iv: London. A street

The new order is under way. Before we get to Westminster, Doll, apparently heavily pregnant, is being taken to prison by two beadles, under fierce protest from Mistress Quickly. The beadle threatens Doll with a belly-whipping; she dares him to make her child miscarry. Mistress Quickly invokes the name of Falstaff – if he were here 'he would make this a bloody day to somebody' – as indeed he surely would. Quickly then fervently prays the opposite of what she means: 'I pray God the fruit of her womb miscarry!' 'If it do,' the beadle drolly replies, 'you shall have a dozen of cushions again; you have but eleven now.' It seems that the women and Pistol have beaten a man, and that he is dead. This comes as something of a surprise, after what we have seen of Doll's relationship with Pistol in the previous scene, but emotions are volatile at the Boar's Head. She and the beadle exchange gutter insults, hers largely dwelling on the thinness and sallowness of his features, his on her profession. It is a hissing, spitting, clawing, shoving, kicking scene, a disturbingly unwholesome prelude to the joyfully anticipated event of the coronation. There is no direct evidence that the city is being cleaned up for the occasion, as in Aleksandr Gelman's *Stars in the Morning Sky*, where the tarts are rounded up off the streets in preparation for the Olympic Games; nor is there a specific drive to extirpate the disreputable, as in *Measure for Measure*; but from its position in the play – it is the penultimate scene – it has a more than circumstantial impact. Law and order are in the ascendant, for better or for worse.

### Scene v: Westminster. Near the Abbey

Grooms are strewing rushes on the ground as the King and his train pass across the stage to the sound of trumpets; behind them are Falstaff, Shallow, Bardolph, Pistol and the Page. Falstaff is in a state of feverish excitement, mingling boasts of his influence with Hal, calculation as to his appearance, and – *pace* certain influential commentators – unmistakably genuine and heartfelt emotion at the prospect of being reunited with the boy. The rhythm and tempo of these exchanges, as Shallow and Pistol spur him on, rises to almost orgasmic levels of excitement:

FALSTAFF  Stand here by me, Master Robert Shallow, I will make the King do you grace. I will leer upon him as a comes by, and do but mark the countenance that he will give me.

PISTOL  God bless thy lungs, good knight!

FALSTAFF  Come here, Pistol, stand behind me. [*To Shallow*] O, if I had had time to have made new liveries, I would have bestowed the thousand pound I borrowed of you. But 'tis no matter, this poor show doth better, this doth infer the zeal I had to see him.

SHALLOW  It doth so.

FALSTAFF  It shows my earnestness of affection.

SHALLOW  It doth so.

FALSTAFF  My devotion –

SHALLOW  It doth, it doth, it doth.

FALSTAFF  As it were, to ride day and night, and not to deliberate, not to remember, not to have patience to shift me –

SHALLOW  It is best, certain.

FALSTAFF  But to stand stained with travel, and sweating with desire to see him, thinking of nothing else, putting all affairs else in oblivion, as if there were nothing else to be done but to see him.

If this is acting, as I have observed elsewhere, it is very good acting in which the feeling is utterly real even though it has its origin in the imagination.

Pistol, perhaps unable to cope with such strong and freely expressed emotion, as opposed to his habitual fustian, is driven to Latin, which receives an approving nod from Shallow (though, as often in his utterances, he has actually said absolutely nothing at all – in this case a translation would roughly run: ''Twas ever thus, there is nothing else, it is the same all the way through') But now he has something important to tell Falstaff, and does so with – for him – some directness:

> My knight, I will inflame thy noble liver,
> And make thee rage.
> Thy Doll, and Helen of thy noble thoughts,
> Is in base durance and contagious prison,
> Hal'd thither
> By most mechanical and dirty hand.
> Rouse up Revenge from ebon den with fell Alecto's snake,
> For Doll is in.

For Falstaff, delirious with anticipated glory and certain advancement, this is no problem: 'I will deliver her.' Trumpets pierce the air. Cheers are heard. Falstaff roars above the crowd in terms of reckless intimacy using the pet name that he himself coined: 'God save thy Grace, King Hal, my royal Hal!' Pistol backs this up with almost equal directness: 'The heavens thee guard and keep, most royal imp of fame!' Falstaff continues with desperate tenderness: 'God save thee, my sweet boy!' The word *lèse-majesté* was coined for just such utterances. The King speaks to the Lord Chief Justice, who is presumably waiting anxiously to see which way the King will jump. This is the ultimate test: faced with the charming reality of the man, will he really be able to resist? But it is King Henry V who speaks, not Hal: 'My Lord Chief Justice, speak to that vain man.' He does not need to be told twice: 'Have you your wits ? Know you what 'tis you speak?' Falstaff, however, is beyond any appeal to sense; he is distracted with adoration. 'My King! My Jove! I speak to thee, my heart!' In response to this passionate avowal, the King speaks six of the most chilling words in the whole of Shakespeare: 'I know thee not, old man.' He seems for a moment genuinely not to know who Falstaff is. 'Fall to thy prayers. / How ill white hairs becomes a fool and jester!' No: he knew him once, but now he knows him not:

> I have long dreamt of such a kind of man,
> So surfeit-swell'd, so old, and so profane;
> But being awak'd I do despise my dream.

Again the language of the sonnets is called to mind: 'Thus have I had thee, as a dream doth flatter: / In sleep a king, but waking, no such matter' (Sonnet 87). Then he urges Falstaff to reform: 'Make less thy body hence, and more thy grace; / Leave gormandising.' For a moment, he seems to hint at the old Boar's Head style of bodily abuse: is this a *joke*, perhaps? 'Know the grave doth gape / For thee thrice wider than for other men.' Certainly Falstaff seems to think there might be an opening for a riposte, but the King cuts him off summarily: 'Reply not to me with a fool-born jest.'

What he says next seems as much destined for the ears of his court and the people as for Falstaff:

> Presume not that I am the thing I was;
> For God doth know, so shall the world perceive,
> That I have turn'd away my former self;
> So will I those that kept me company.

Then he turns the full blast of his icy words on Falstaff again:

When thou dost hear I am as I have been,
Approach me, and thou shalt be as thou wast,
The tutor and the feeder of my riots.

Clearly this is intended pejoratively, and yet the word 'tutor'
tells us that Hal has learned something from the man he is
now so publicly rejecting. 'Till then I banish thee, on pain of
death, / As I have done the rest of my misleaders' – a cruel
touch: Falstaff is not even the principal misleader, simply one
among many – 'Not to come near our person by ten mile.'
Here the Christian view of hell springs to mind, in which the
punishment of the damned is simply to be denied the Divine
Presence. At a less metaphysical level, it also means that, as
long as the King is in London, Falstaff is barred from the
Boar's Head, an only slightly less dreadful fate. Inexorably,
Henry V continues his judgement, for all the world as if he
were on the bench in the High Court of Law; he has indeed, as
he promised, assumed the voice of the Lord Chief Justice:

For competence of life I will allow you,
That lack of means enforce you not to evils;
And as we hear you do reform yourselves,
We will, according to your strengths and qualities,
Give you advancement.

Reform himself! A reformed Falstaff – as he has often enough
suggested himself – is an absurdity, as absurd as a Christian
Shylock. So there will be no advancement for Falstaff. To
clinch the absoluteness of the judgement, the King entrusts its
execution to Falstaff's nemesis, the Lord Chief Justice: 'Be it
your charge, my lord, / To see perform'd the tenor of my word.'
Then, with a brisk instruction – 'Set on' – he is gone.

The public world moves away and the little group is left
alone onstage. Falstaff – so untypically silent for so long –

faces an inevitable fact: 'Master Shallow, I owe you a thousand pound.' Shallow, sharply focused, no longer the circular chatterbox we have up till now known him to be, is brisk in his reply: 'Yea, marry, Sir John, which I beseech you to let me have home with me.' Falstaff is equally brisk in response: 'That can hardly be, Master Shallow.' Then, casually, he adds: 'Do not you grieve at this; I shall be sent for in private to him'; and he has a perfect explanation. The great escapologist, though not so nimbly, perhaps, as in other circumstances, is still capable of slipping away when he seems cornered. 'Look you, he must seem thus to the world. Fear not your advancements; I will be the man yet that shall make you great.' Shallow has a tart and unkind response to that: 'I cannot perceive how, unless you give me your doublet, and stuff me out with straw. I beseech you, good Sir John, let me have five hundred of my thousand.' He knows enough of Falstaff to recognize that any hope of getting the whole sum is doomed. 'Sir, I will be as good as my word,' replies Falstaff, resuming some of his former grandeur. 'This that you heard was but a colour [a feint].' Shallow will allow him to get away with nothing: 'A colour' – with a pun on 'collar'; that is, the hangman's noose – 'that I fear you will die in, Sir John.' But Falstaff continues in lordly fashion: 'Fear no colours' – a proverbial phrase meaning that one should fear no enemies. 'Go with me to dinner. Come, Lieutenant Pistol; come, Bardolph.' Then a final confidence that is heartbreaking in its simplicity: 'I shall be sent for soon at night.' Perhaps he believes that he will be smuggled into the palace at Westminster and things will resume just as they were at the beginning of *Henry IV, Part I* when he and Hal were 'squires of the night's body' and 'the moon's men'. Over dinner, he will no doubt expand on these matters.

He has, however, utterly misjudged the world in which he now finds himself. The Lord Chief Justice and Prince John suddenly appear with officers. 'Go carry Sir John Falstaff to the Fleet,' commands the lawman. 'Take all his company along with him.' 'My lord, my lord, –' cries Falstaff, the last words we are ever to hear him utter. The Lord Chief Justice cuts him short. 'I cannot now speak: I will hear you soon. / Take them away.' Pistol gives vent to one last exclamation in Latin, and they are all – including, presumably, Shallow and the Page – swept away to prison, as if to underline the practical force of the King's judgement. Left alone, the Prince and the Lord Chief Justice rejoice in the new order: the King has been firm but fair in the matter of Falstaff and his gang. He has, too, called parliament. The dying King's advice is being followed to the letter, to John's entire satisfaction:

> I will lay odds that, ere this year expire,
> We bear our civil swords and native fire
> As far as France. I heard a bird so sing,
> Whose music, to my thinking, pleas'd the King.

This will have come as no surprise to the Elizabethan audience, to whom the glories of Agincourt were a golden memory of England at its most triumphant. Nor, surely, would they have been in the least critical of the policy of waging foreign war to unite the nation. Yet even that audience may have felt that ending the play with its two most rigid, humourless and uncompromising characters in such a state of ascendancy and smug satisfaction, while Falstaff, Pistol, Bardolph and Shallow, whose abundant life and appetite have proved so touching, diverting, and invigorating, are incarcerated, is not a deeply satisfying outcome. It may be that, even for them, as for us, the spectacle of Falstaff crying 'My lord, my lord' as he is bundled off is the image that lingers in the mind. Is a world that has no place for Falstaff and his crew such a splendid place after all? There is no doubt that England now has a king well able to rule, one who, thanks to the breadth of his experience at every level of society, will understand his people better than his predecessors, confined as they were to the court, mired in factional strife and haunted by dynastic concerns; but surely something important has been lost? Something to do with orchards and inns, with booze and sex, with cunning and cheek – the spirit of playfulness, of anarchy, of desire, something pagan and of the body and of nature, welling up from the deepest, darkest, most creative places in the human soul? Something essential?

That sense of loss hangs in the air, persisting in the mind after the play has ended, outlasting the memory even of the glorious and necessary transformation of Hal into Henry V, and banishing all thought of the Lord Chief Justice and Prince John, believing that they have stitched everything up, glowing with urbane self-congratulation, as they leave the stage to inhabit the new world so pleasingly shaped in their own image: 'Come, will you hence ?'

# Epilogue

It is generally agreed by editors that the Epilogue as printed is a conflation of three possible speeches. It bears little relevance to the play we have just seen, although it has a certain charm in that it represents a mode of Elizabethan public speaking, almost like an after-dinner speech, chatty, humorous and a little informative; in this particular example, as a bonus, the speaker executes a jig. The end of the speech plugs the next play in the sequence ('If you be not too much cloyed with fat meat . . .'), and it is in this section of the speech that the greatest interest lies for us: promising to continue the story, he also promises more of Falstaff who, 'for anything I know . . . shall die of a sweat' in France, 'unless already a be killed with your hard opinions' (provoking cries, presumably, of 'No, no' from its first audience). Doffing his cap in the direction of the family of Lord Cobham, the Lord Chamberlain, which was related to Sir John Oldcastle, the speaker unequivocally states: 'Oldcastle died martyr, and this is not the man.' After which the speaker signs off with a last jig: 'My tongue is weary; when my legs are too, I will bid you good night.'

Of course Falstaff, for whatever reason, does not return in *Henry V*, although his death is memorably reported in it. This completes Falstaff's story, so I shall discuss it in an appendix. The Falstaff of *The Merry Wives of Windsor* is a different matter – a sort of sitcom spin-off. The play is of great interest – Shakespeare's only bourgeois play – but the character of Falstaff, bereft both of his career and of his environment, dwindles to a mere character, quite lacking the mythic resonances that have been so much the subject of the present volume and its predecessor. He can be funny and sometimes even touching, but he becomes simply an aristocratic sponger and con man, vain and venal: there is no splendour, no majesty. It is a glimpse of what a more or less reformed Falstaff, banished from Eastcheap and stripped of his soldierly functions, might have been like. It is not an edifying sight.

# Appendix

## The Death of Falstaff: *Henry V*, Act II, scenes i and iii

From the first immortally exuberant words of the Prologue, *Henry V* breathes a different air from its two great predecessors. The dank, doom-laden anguish and exhaustion of the court scenes are replaced by energy, enterprise and a sense of possibility. Hal is 'war-like Harry'; his astonishing overnight transformation from reckless and rebellious youth to King 'full of grace and fair regard' is compared by the Bishop of Ely to the growth of strawberries under nettles: 'wholesome berries thrive and ripen best / Neighbour'd by fruit of baser quality'. Growth is a key phrase, in implicit contrast to the earlier plays' constant reference to mortality. The 'unletter'd, rude and shallow' companions of Henry's recent past have been rooted up and cast away. England rejoices at the new atmosphere of hope and self-confidence, preparing for a war with France that will restore the King to the throne of France, which he and his courtiers have convinced themselves is by rights his. Even the old Eastcheap crowd are actively and enthusiastically preparing for war, though they have lost nothing of their former disputatiousness. Pistol and Nym are sworn enemies and a sword fight threatens to break out between them. Pistol has married Mistress Quickly – rather surprisingly, given her insistently repeated aversion to swaggerers. His old hostility to Doll Tearsheet holds good, though, as he savagely recommends her as a wife to Nym:

> ... from the powdering-tub of infamy
> Fetch forth the lazar kite of Cressid's kind,
> Doll Tearsheet she by name, and her espouse.

These pleasantries are interrupted by the arrival of Falstaff's Boy, who calls on Pistol and Quickly to attend his master: 'he is very sick, and would to bed.' The witty boy attempts a Bardolph joke – 'put thy face between his sheets and do the office of a warming-pan' – but then, lest there should be any doubt about the seriousness of the situation, he soberly repeats himself: 'Faith, he's very ill.' Bardolph sends the boy off with a flea in his ear, and Quickly predicts that he'll end up on the gallows ('he'll yield the crow a pudding one of these days'); but she knows that he is telling the truth. 'The King has killed his heart,' she says, in a phrase that pulls us straight back to the terrible scene of Falstaff's rejection and casts a shadow on the new King's radiance. She urges Pistol to follow on, and leaves with the boy. Pistol and Nym resume their altercation regardless, with Bardolph in the role of mediator, but they are interrupted by the returning Quickly, who has been alarmed by what she's seen. As usual under pressure, her grasp of sense collapses: 'Ah, poor heart! He is so shak'd of a burning quotidian tertian, that is most lamentable to behold.' She urges the men to follow, and they do, and as they leave, they are in no doubt as to where to lay the blame for what has happened: 'The King hath run bad humours on the knight; that's the even of it.' Pistol concurs: Falstaff's heart is 'fracted and corroborate' – Pistolese, presumably, for 'broken and corrupted'. Nym presses on with his criticism of the king's behaviour and his capriciousness – 'the King is a good king: but it must be as it may; he passes some humours and careers' – which constitutes a further small diminution of the golden aura with which he has been almost universally endowed so far. Pistol urges them to go and 'condole the knight', but with the cheerful realism of comedy, he adds 'for, lambkins, we will live'.

We next see the same King in the vigorous exercise of statecraft, making an example of the traitors Scroop, Grey and

Cambridge, who, having decried his leniency towards some drunken revellers who abused him, turn their lack of mercy against themselves. Effective, brisk, witty, he is already a King of action and authority: 'Cheerly to sea; the signs of war advance: / No king of England, if not king of France.'

Meanwhile Falstaff has died.

The scene is a London street, outside a tavern – the Boar's Head, presumably. Quickly is keen to accompany Pistol to Southampton on his way to France, but he will have none of it: he needs to mourn Falstaff: 'No; for my manly heart doth earn [grieve],' Bardolph cries: 'Would I were with him, wheresome'er he is, either in heaven or hell!' 'Nay, sure,' rejoins Quickly, 'he's not in hell: he's in Arthur's bosom, if ever man went to Arthur's bosom.' Commentators generally assume that she has fallen into another verbal hole in the ground, and that she really means Abraham's bosom, as in the parable of Dives and Lazarus, a favourite of Falstaff's; but there is a possibility that for once she means what she says, and that it is the king of Ancient Britain whom he is imagined to join, rather than the Old Testament patriarch. For all his parsonical posings, Falstaff belongs not to the Judaeo-Christian tradition, but to the pagan past. Quickly's death-bed report is expectedly full of sensuous detail and folk wisdom, a fine example of her undiscriminating total recall. He made a fine end, she says, and compares him to a 'christom child' – a recently baptized baby – recalling Falstaff's own account of his birth: 'My lord, I was born about three of the clock in the afternoon, with a white head, and something a round belly.' He died between twelve and one – 'ev'n at the turning o' th' tide' – a good traditional time at which to die; she saw him 'fumble with the sheets and play with flowers and smile upon his fingers' end'. The absolute reality of this gives us the man in his situation with photographic precision. She immediately knew from this evidence that 'there was but

one way'. It seems that he has died not of any of the conse-
quences of his disgraceful life, but of the plague. His nose was –
as you would expect if you had read your Hippocrates – 'as
sharp as a pen' and 'a babbled of green fields'. She called out to
him to be of good cheer, but he simply shouted 'God, God,
God!' over and over, despite her reassurances that such
thoughts were premature. He asked for blankets to be placed on
his feet, she says. Then, with professional skill, she explored his
body: 'I put my hand into the bed and felt them [his feet], and
they were cold as any stone; then I felt to his knees, and so
upward, and upward, and all was as cold as any stone.'

Several commentators have noted that this description
echoes the famous description of Socrates's death from Plato's
*Phaedo*:

> The man – he was the same one who had administered the
> poison – kept his hand upon Socrates, and after a little
> while examined his feet and legs, then pinched his foot
> hard and asked if he felt it, Socrates said no. Then he did
> the same to his legs, and moving gradually upward in this
> way, let us see that he was getting cold and numb.
> Presently he felt him again and said that when it reached
> the heart Socrates would be gone. The coldness was
> spreading about as far as his waist [groin] when Socrates
> uncovered his face, for he had covered it up, and said –
> they were his last words – 'Crito, we ought to offer a cock
> to Asclepius. See to it, and don't forget.' 'No, it shall be
> done,' said Crito. 'Are you sure that there is nothing else?'
> Socrates made no reply to this question, but after a little
> while he stirred, and when the man uncovered him, his
> eyes were fixed. When Crito saw this, he closed the mouth
> and eyes.*

* Translated by Hugh Tredennick.

It is a little difficult to know how Shakespeare might have come across this passage, since in his day it was only available in Greek and Latin, with which – as Ben Jonson delighted to report – he had only nodding acquaintance; but there are striking parallels between Falstaff and the Athenian philosopher, which Michael Platt has listed:

> While impersonating his father, Prince Hal himself called Falstaff 'That villainous abominable misleader of youth' (*I Henry IV*, II, iv, 439) . . . the very charge often made against Socrates, and one of the two formal charges brought against him by Meletus, Anytus, and Lycon. Like Socrates, Falstaff is accused of making the worse appear the better reason. Falstaff is always asking Socratic questions, of the type: What is a thing? With them he, like Socrates, examines things and disturbs people. With his question, What is honour?, Falstaff calls into question the life of the gentleman. With his deeds and speeches and laughter, he seems to ask, What is courage? the very question which arises when Socrates meets with the distinguished generals Laches and Nioas in the Laches. Like Socrates, Falstaff serves in his country's armies and, like Socrates, he serves on foot rather than on horse: Falstaff says he is witty and the cause of wit in other men (*2 Henry IV*, I, ii, 6): the friends of Socrates think that he is wise and the cause of wisdom in themselves. Falstaff drinks much, and so can Socrates. Neither Falstaff nor Socrates is beautiful, yet both exercise an extraordinary attraction upon other men. Together with their deaths, all these resemblances show that Shakespeare likens Falstaff to Socrates.

Though its direct application in performance is not immediately evident, this is a very suggestive notion.

The anthropologist Roderick Marshall notes that Socrates is insistently compared to the god Silenos, tutor of Dionysos, and here we may see a strong connection between the god, the Athenian and the Englishman. Alcibiades, Socrates's pupil and lover – Dionysos to his Silenos – is speaking:

Is (Socrates) not like a Silenos in this? To be sure he is: this outer mask is the carved head of the Silenos; but O my companions in drink, when he is opened, what temperance there is residing within! Know you that luxury and wealth and *honour*, at which the many wonder, are of no account with him and are utterly despised by him . . . All his life is spent at mocking and flouting at those who pursue them. But when I opened him, and looked within at his serious purposes, I saw in him divine and golden images of such fascinating beauty that I did in a moment whatever Socrates commanded.

Whether Falstaff is found to contain divine and golden images is questionable, but certainly he is bursting with life energy – until, of course, the moment of death; yet there seems to have been a meaning in that, too. As Marshall writes:

Plain Jack Falstaff of course rose to no . . . philosophical heights on his death-bed, yet he did play with flowers and babble happily of green fields while his motley followers roistered in the tap room below and Hal, now Henry V, who under the hand (and thumb) of Old Father Antic had rejected and in one way or another killed him, was at last enabled – perhaps by his mysterious tutor's mysterious death – to sail for France and give the *coup de grâce* to a still wobbling Turkish Knight. And thereby he turned the pleasaunce which Richard and his murderer had allowed to become choked with weeds back into a place of peace and plenty, to which he added 'the world's best garden', France.

The point, of course, is that something extraordinary has gone out of the world with his death. After Quickly has spoken, the others chip in, though there is no more agreement about him after death than there was during life. Nym tells us that he denounced sack; Bardolph claims that he denounced women, which Mistress Quickly denies; but the boy takes Bardolph's side: Falstaff said they were 'devils incarnate', provoking Quickly to recollect, surreally, that 'A never could abide carnation; 'twas a colour he never lik'd.' The boy persists in reporting Falstaff's death-bed rejection of the female sex; she concedes that he may have been out of sorts with women, but only because of the rheumatism that caused him to prate of the Whore of Babylon. The boy fondly recalls a vintage Bardolph joke of his master's: a flea stuck on his nose, which Falstaff said was 'a black soul burning in hell'. With a melancholy grumble, Bardolph notes that the fuel for the fire – booze – has gone now: it was the only wages he ever got from the old bugger. At which Nym says, 'Shall we shog?' and it's all over: they pass on to the future; but the scene is so vivid as to constitute another Falstaff scene, perhaps the greatest of them all. His death gives him life.

There is no further mention of Falstaff throughout the play, but the scene creates a memorable atmosphere that adds a deep-resonating harmony to the bright and brilliant proceedings of Hal triumphant. It is difficult to imagine Falstaffian follies interweaving with the heroics of Agincourt, as promised by the author: there is comedy there, to be sure, but not of the wickedly subversive kind that Falstaff purveyed. Yet how could Hal have acquired the touch of Harry in the night, his ability to pass among and understand his soldiers, without the extensive education he received in Eastcheap? The spirit of the Boar's Head lives, even though its supreme expression has been silenced.

# Bibliography

The field of scholarship relating to *Henry IV, Parts I and II* is exceptionally rich and stimulating. It will be apparent from a reading of this book that I owe a great debt to three writers in particular: C. L. Barber, Graham Holderness and, most provocatively, Roderick Marshall; but each book on the following list is well worth study, Bloom's compendium on Falstaff himself being an especially wide-ranging survey of that roundest of men.

Auden, W. H., *Lectures on Shakespeare*, 2000.

Bakhtin, Mikhail, *Rabelais and His World*, 1968.

Barber, C. L., *Shakespeare's Festive Comedy*, 1959.

Barber, C. L. and Richard P. Wheeler, *The Whole Journey*, 1986.

Bloom, Harold J. (ed.), *Falstaff*, 1992.

Brody, Alan, *The English Mummers and their Plays*, 1969.

Charlton, H. B., *Shakespearian Comedy*, 1938.

Duffy, Eamon, *The Stripping of the Altars*, 1992.

Empson, William, *Some Versions of Pastoral*, 1935.

Hodgson, Beryl, *The Bedford Companion to Henry IV, Part I*, 1997.

Holderness, Graham, *Shakespeare's History*, 1985.

Humphreys, A. R. (ed.), *King Henry IV, Part 1*, 1960.

Hunter, Greek, *King Henry IV, Parts 1 & 2, Casebook*, 1970.

Hutton, Ronald, *The Rise and Fall of Merry England*, 1994.

Marshall, Roderick, *Falstaff the Archetypal Myth*, 1989.

Rhodes, Neil, *Elizabethan Grotesque*, 1980.

Tiddy, R. J. E. *The Mummers' Plays*, 1923.

Tillyard, E. M. W. *Shakespeare's History Plays*, 1944.

Torrance, Robert M., *The Comic Hero*, 1978.
Tynan, Kenneth, *He That Plays the King*, 1950.
Wilson, J. Dover, *The Fortunes of Falstaff*, 1943.
Wilson, J. Dover (ed.), *King Henry IV, Part I*, 1946.